An Indefinite Period

A Memoir about Family Life on the
Guantanamo Bay Naval Base
During the Cuban Missile Crisis of 1962

By

Patricia Hale Feeney

ISBN 0-7414-1212-8

Published by:

PUBLISHING.COM

519 West Lancaster Avenue
Haverford, PA 19041-1413
Info@buybooksontheweb.com
www.buybooksontheweb.com
Toll-free (877) BUY BOOK
Local Phone (610) 520-2500
Fax (610) 519-0261

Printed in the United States of America

Printed on Recycled Paper

Published September, 2002

For my children

Colleen Patricia Hollenbeck

William Fabian Kendig, Jr.

John James Kendig

who have not only sustained me since they came into my life, but in the conduct of their lives, have provided me with a constant source of inspiration and pride.

ACKNOWLEDGEMENTS

My lifetime friend, Patricia Ward Atherholt, performed a meticulous first reading of my memoir. Her perceptive comments and corrections contributed enormously to the finished product.

Susan Buck, creator of quasi-intellectual, semi-sarcastic essays, performed an additional vigilant edit. Many thanks, Susan, for your discerning observations and opinions.

I am also indebted to Graphics Designers Shawn S. Copley, Gus Pennock, and Douglas C. Soule. Their professionalism and artistry made it possible to include historic photographs in this document.

Always and most fervently, I have been blessed with the patience and support of my husband, Dennis William Durham. Without his encouragement and computer expertise, this publication would not have been possible.

Bio photo on back cover courtesy of Mary Katherine (Taffy) Hale.

CONTENTS

CONTENTS

PROLOGUE

On October 22, 1962, the history of mankind came "as close to Armageddon as it has ever come".[1] This memoir is not another chronicle of the military and diplomatic issues of the Cuban Missile Crisis. It is a personal account, concerning how this epic event affected the military families living on the Guantanamo Bay Naval Base at that time, and in particular, how it affected me and my children, ages 2 and 3.

My children and I had received orders to accompany their father, a Marine officer, on his two-year tour of duty at the Naval Base. Marines were responsible for keeping Guantanamo in a garrison position to enable the Navy to safely conduct their training exercises.

How much did I know about the evolving drama that threatened my life and the lives of my children? And, how did it feel to be evacuated from my home and thrust without warning into the role of a displaced person? Although none of us knew it that hot October day, we were living history. We were President Kennedy's last impediment to action. With us evacuated from the Naval Base, he would be free to call Khrushchev's bluff!

Throughout this exodus, I describe my obsession to create a sense of sanctuary for my travel-weary children. All I wanted was to go home . . . and I didn't even know where that was.

Given current telecommunications expertise, it is almost incomprehensible to appreciate how little we in Guantanamo knew. We were unaware that the United States was in the middle of a missile crisis and that we were at ground zero. We had no information about the transformation of Castro's Cuba into a nuclear bastion with Russian armaments aimed at America's belly.

Since the world is still managing the debris of the October Crisis of 1962, the emotional climate described in these pages is not only timely, but ripe. Castro's ongoing indignation about American occupation of the Naval Base at Guantanamo continues to be an underlying deterrent to contemporary US-Cuba rapprochement. Additionally, the evolving events recounted in my memoir contain many of the same impassioned components that provoked the 9/11/01 terrorist Attack on America, such as occupants of a smaller country feeling righteous indignation and hostility toward a larger and more affluent one.

The sands of time are running out for those of us who had a front row seat on the Cuban Missile Crisis. It is clear the full story has yet to be told. My story is a quest for *home*, evoking one woman's attempt to make sense of a world that does not always make sense and presenting an intimate insight into this human drama still in search of an acceptable denouement.

---

[1] Wyden, Peter, <u>Bay of Pigs, The Untold Story</u> – Simon and Schuster, NY, 1979 – A quote attributed to CIA Director, William E. Colby, 7.

"Where to start is the problem, because nothing begins when it begins and nothing's over when it's over... History is a construct... Any point of entry is possible and all choices are arbitrary. Still, there are definitive moments, moments we use as references, because they break our sense of continuity, they change the direction of time. We can look at these events and we can say that after them things were never the same again."

- *Margaret Atwood*
  The Robber Bride
  1993

1

Our New Home

The home contained eleven spacious rooms. In each was a ceiling fan like those in the movie "Casablanca". If that wasn't enough, our yard resembled a Garden of Eden. To cap it all off, the aqua waters of the Guantanamo Bay shimmered just beyond the rock wall in our back yard.

My husband, Marine Captain William F. Kendig, had arrived on the Naval Base at Guantanamo Bay, Cuba July 10, 1962 to begin his assignment as Supply Officer of the Marine Barracks, which included providing the troops in a garrison position with food, clothing, and shelter. It was the last day of July when I, along with our children, Billy-2, and Colleen-3, received orders to join him.

Our welcome to Cuba was the grandest I'd ever experienced. After landing at the McCalla Field Naval Air Station (Leeward Point, as it was called), we were conveyed across the Bay in the gig of the Commanding Officer of the Marine Barracks, Colonel George W. Killen. At the pier on the Winward side, we were greeted by the families of all eight Marine officers stationed there.

The quarters assigned to us had already been converted into 'home', courtesy of the combined efforts of our nearest neighbors and their Cuban domestic help. Our household effects were unpacked, sheets were on the beds, pictures were hung, and fresh flowers graced the living room. There was a roast in the oven, and the refrigerator was stocked with basic essentials, as well as a bottle of chilling champagne.

Excerpts of an early letter I wrote to my family in Salt Lake City, Utah follows:

August 8, 1962

Dear Mom, Dad and Jack,

Had to think carefully to even remember the date. We've done so much since arrival I can't believe it was only a week ago.

Thursday last we went to a cocktail party at the SeaBee Club. It was lovely and I met the wonderful men who have been helping Bill since his arrival, so we decided to have a dinner party for them on Friday.

We borrowed Viola, the neighbor's maid (born in St. Johns, Virgin Islands). She set up the buffet, made a lovely floral arrangement on each table, served the coffee, cleared the tables, did up all the dishes, and put away any leftover food.

Kay Seibert, 14 year-old daughter of our neighbors, minded the kids. She took them to her house to watch TV, since our TV isn't hooked up yet.

Saturday, the Marines gave us a Welcome Aboard party. They give one to each Marine officer/wife who arrives or leaves. Since there are only eight Marine officers here, they tend to stick together. It was a lovely barbeque in the yard of Kay Seibert's folks, Claire and Lt. Colonel Kenneth D. Seibert.

Tuesday morning, Bill strapped on his keys, buckled on his gun belt, and assumed the duty guard of Gitmo, which is the local nick-name for Guantanamo. It takes three and a half hours to check the guard posts on the fence line, and he must do that twice during the 24-hour guard duty. As he does so, sometimes the Cuban militiamen, guarding their side of the fence, wave or take pictures of him. It's morosely humorous.

Right now, Claire and Ken are on the USNS *Geiger* heading for a weekend in Panama. All it costs is meals aboard ship (about $4.50 each per day). In about 6 or 8 months, Bill and I hope to make this trip.

This house is a dream. Kids are well and happy, as are we. Hope all is well with you. Do write soon! The kids and I miss you.

P.S. Today, a 'maid' was brought to our back door. . . only she's not really a maid. Can only say she is being sought by the Castro Revolutionary government, and we are pretending she is our maid to save her life. I'm not making this up! She is only 24-years-old, and very attractive - a college graduate who taught high school in Cuba.

Life here is anything but dull!

Love always, Pat

Welcome to

GUANTANAMO BAY - U.S. NAVAL BASE

1-1   New home . . . shown by door is author's daughter, Colleen, at age 3

1-2   Captain William F. Kendig with his children Colleen and Billy, ages 3 and 2

1-3   Guantanamo Bay as seen from backyard of author's new home
with "X" indicating ships on maneuvers.

2

The Exile

In an earlier and more relaxed time, the flow of workers from the interior of Cuba to the Naval Base was constant and easy, but because of the stringent requirements imposed on Cuban nationals by President Fidel Castro in January of 1961 (a pass required for entry; searches at the gate; conversion of 90% of their pay to Cuban pesos), there was a severe shortage of domestic help by the time we arrived.

It was advisable to hire a maid because the Base quarters were extremely large.   Also, fine silt was continually blowing through the wooden louvers, which were devoid of glass. Unless the 11 rooms were kept mopped daily, this silt would build up, and each step would render it airborne for a final resting place on counter tops, tables, and in food.

I investigated hiring a maid when we first arrived and put my name on a waiting list.   Only those Cuban Nationals who were already employed on the Base and had a work pass issued by Castro's Revolutionary Army were allowed through the gate. It was necessary to wait until a family returned to the United States and relinquished their maid for one to become available.   I was told it might be months before this would happen.

Therefore, I was extremely delighted when my husband called one August afternoon and told me a Marine Sergeant by the name of Alvarez would be bringing me a maid.
"Please don't tell anyone," he added.

I could not understand the need for secrecy, but I was so delighted at the prospect of having help to tame the dust that I readily agreed.

Shortly thereafter, Sergeant Alvarez appeared at our back door with a young woman. I took note of the fact that he had driven in his own beat-up vehicle rather than a military jeep. He introduced Mierna Suarez to me, then turning to her, he made his introduction of me in Spanish.

Mierna was tall and beautifully groomed. She had on high heels and a fashionable dress of obvious quality. She certainly didn't look like the Cuban maids I'd seen around the neighborhood wearing kerchiefs around their heads and obviously homemade clothing.

The Sergeant spoke a few words to Mierna in Spanish, and motioned for her to go into our kitchen and have a seat at the table. I followed her in and sat down with her. Behind us, I heard the door close as the Sergeant left.

The Sergeant's car had barely driven out of our driveway when Mierna put her head down on the table, cradled it in her arms, and began to wail. She did not just cry or sob. She keened and occasionally punctuated the air with a loud, piercing scream, accompanied by a pounding of her fist on the table.

My children, who had been playing in another room, came and stood tentatively in the doorway. I was so dumbfounded I couldn't move. Gradually, the children crept in and clung to me. Even if I'd known why Mierna was crying, it would have been difficult for me to offer any comfort when I didn't speak her language. I was afraid that whatever I might do would only make matters worse.

There seemed no let-up in the well of her misery, whatever it was, and we all remained frozen for some minutes before I could even recover enough to reassure the children. I put my arms around them, and said we would make the nice lady a cup of tea. It was then I noticed the suitcase that Sergeant Alvarez had inconspicuously left in our back entryway when he departed.

I put the kettle on to boil as best I could with the children still clinging to my legs, and crossed the room to the wall phone to call my husband.
"Honey", I tried to say quietly over the wailing, "This 'maid' that Sergeant Alvarez left on our doorstep is crying nonstop."
My husband could not avoid hearing Mierna's lamentations in the background. There was a slight pause, and he said,
"I'll be right home."
This further alarmed me. It was 2:00 in the afternoon. Neither fever nor flood had ever compelled my Marine to come home in the middle of the afternoon.

Since no place on the 45-square miles of the Base was very distant, it was not long before Bill arrived and found me tending the tea water. Mierna remained as before. Bill quietly led me past Mierna, through the dining room, and into the front room. The kids followed, still clinging to me. My husband sat down on the couch, and pulled me down next to him with the children huddled around us.
"This woman is a prisoner in our home", Bill began.
"Her life is in danger. No one is to know she is here," he continued.

Apparently, Mierna's husband had been one of the Cuban organizers of the failed invasion at the Bay of

8

Pigs (April 1961). No one knew whether he was alive or dead. There had been threats on Mierna's life in Cuba from revolutionary leaders, so she had asked for asylum on the Base. Some of the Cubans on the Base were also not sympathetic to her husband's cause, and when they found out who she was, her life was in danger from them.

Mierna had escaped the Cuban barracks and sought asylum with the Marines who dared not keep her with them. Military personnel were warned not to take sides in any issues between Cuban personnel on the Base. When my husband heard about this, he suggested they sneak her out of the barracks and bring her to our home, a somewhat more neutral territory. Military personnel would be trying to arrange her passage to Florida as soon as possible. My heart nearly burst with anguish for this poor woman, and I told my husband I understood and would take care of it. He had to leave before his being home in the middle of the day should arouse suspicion.

After Bill left, I finished brewing the tea and put the pot and cups on the table near Mierna. I gave the children cookies and milk at their small table. Then I went into my bedroom and grabbed my manicure kit. Without language, I knew this would be a difficult encounter.

Sitting down across from Mierna, I began to take the polish off my nails. The fumes were enough to at least get her attention. As she raised her head from the table, I handed her tissues, and gestured toward the teapot. She swiped at her eyes, and nodded assent to a cup of tea. I had taken down the dainty china cups and brought out the Sterling silver, as a gesture of respect and hospitality. When I offered sugar, she took several spoons full. This, I was soon to learn, was the habit of all Cubans. After all, it was their native product.

We sipped our tea. When I smiled and reached for her hand, she let me take it and smiled back. Soon we were both involved in manicuring our nails, asking each other's approval of color choice. All this was possible without language, because grooming is the universal language of women everywhere.

Before my husband arrived home for dinner, we were 'conversing'. She would touch an object and repeat the Spanish word for it, and I would repeat it, trying to replicate her accent. Then, I would do the same in English. I learned that she was 24 years old, and before her marriage, had lived with her family in a 'grand casa' (described with arms outstretched) with seven servants (with seven fingers raised). Her father was an official with the Cuban government (not the Castro Revolutionary Army), and she had been a highschool teacher. Her husband and brother were both Colonels in the Cuban government forces, not the Castro regime.

Mierna spoke with tears in her eyes about how the Castro regime had driven her family from their 'grande casa', had confiscated their chickens and most of their possessions. During the planning stages of the Bay of Pigs, she was a newlywed and lived with her husband and five other Cuban exiles in a small, one bedroom house. With exaggerated gestures, she conveyed how she had gone to several different stores and purchased small quantities of food at each in order not raise suspicion that there were seven people living in this house. All but she and her husband slept on the floor.

With flailing gestures, Mierna described the difficulty of learning to cook for seven people when she had never cooked before in her life. She talked of the constant fear of being discovered, and she told with keen emotion about her husband and the men leaving before dawn one April morning in 1961 to participate in the sea and land attack at the Bay of Pigs. She had not heard from or about him since. After that, her life had been sheer terror, most of it spent hiding from anyone who might connect her with her husband's conspiracy against the Castro regime. This time we cried together, with our arms around each other. An understanding between women who love military men transcended language difficulties!

Later that evening, I showed Mierna to her own room in the maid's quarters above our garage. During the second day of her visit, since we were confined to the house, the children served as a welcome distraction for her. She spent most of the time playing with them.

In the afternoon, while the children napped, we shampooed each other's hair and experimented with different ways of styling it, laughing at some of the outlandish possibilities. Mierna brought some of the implements used in her native land to this endeavor, and it was fun to see the differences and similarities between our methods.

By that evening, my husband said the military had arranged that a small airplane would be coming from Florida to fly Mierna off the base. Her take-off time was 9:30 p.m. After dinner, she and I sat on the couch and held hands for most of the evening. I learned she had never flown before. She shared her fear of this with me before she went up to pack.

When Mierna came down with her suitcase, she took my hands in hers and put in them a necklace and matching errings. They were chunky costume jewelry, black beads surrounded by an imitation gold trim, very much in keeping with her style. I tried to protest, as I

11

knew her only possessions from home were this one small suitcase, but I knew they were all she had to offer, and she wanted to present me with something in return for our hospitality. I put them on, thanked her, and gave her a hug. Then I presented her with a package of gum, explaining with exaggerated chewing gestures how she was to chew the gum during the flight to keep her ears from hurting. She seemed to understand, nodded, and put the gum in her purse. Then we heard a car in the driveway.

Sergeant Alvarez had come in his own old car again for obvious reasons. We walked out together, and she asked him how many passengers would be on the plane. He told her she would be the only passenger. She looked terrified, and turned and clung to me. I held her as tenderly as I could. When I pulled away, I made the sign of the cross on her forehead, a gesture signifying a mutual spiritual understanding.

After they drove away, Bill and I sat outside until we saw the lights of a small plane take off from McCalla Field, clearly visible from our backyard. We watched until the blinking identification lights were out of sight, and I said a silent prayer for the future of this young woman whose life had been suddenly and severely altered through circumstances over which she had no control.

Nearly 40 years later, when I encounter Mierna's necklace and earrings among my jewelry, I wonder why I am still keeping them when they are nothing I would ever wear. I take them out, run them through my fingers, and even put them on before returning them to their place. I know I could never bring myself to get rid of them.

2-1 Exile Mierna Suarez, in backyard of author's Gitmo home

2-2 Cuban employees line up for admittance through the gate for a day of work on the Naval Base

3

Reality Check

Guantanamo Bay is considered the ideal Naval training base in the world. There are few days in any year when Naval exercises have to be curtailed because of weather. It has served the United States well to have access to such a facility.

The history of U.S. involvement in this ideal training base goes back nearly a century. In 1903, shortly after the end of the Spanish-American war, a lease agreement on the land occupied by the Naval Base was negotiated between the U.S. and the newly formed Republic of Cuba. It granted the U.S. a total of 28,817 acres, approximately 9,000 of which were covered by water.

Agreements of the 1903 lease of the Naval Base still prevailed at the time of our arrival and included the following: Vessels engaging in Cuban trade had free passage through the waters mentioned in the grants; the U.S. agreed that no private enterprise would operate within the Base; fugitives from justice charged with crimes in Cuba were to be delivered by the U.S. to Cuban authorities; and fugitives from justice charged with crimes on the Base were to be delivered by Order to U.S. authorities. The 1903 document also stipulated that the U.S. would pay a rental of $2,000 per year in gold for the leased area, which was equivalent to $3,386 in 1962. The Navy estimated the value of this installation to be 70 million dollars in 1962.

Another treaty, negotiated and signed in 1934, had the effect of giving the U.S. a perpetual lease on Guantanamo Naval Base, with the provision that it could only be voided by mutual consent between the two countries or by the U.S. abandoning the area. Thus the U.S. had exercised full control over the Naval Base for nearly 60 years when we arrived, although sovereignty still rested with Cuba. All of these agreements, and the very existence of a foreign foothold on Cuban territory, were being used by Fidel Castro in his campaign to breed resentment toward the U.S.

U.S. occupation of the Naval Base was not the only thing for which there was long-standing resentment by Castro and his sympathizers. While Americans have been taught that the U.S. intervention in the Spanish-American War liberated Cuba from Spain, Cubans are convinced the U.S. intervened at the end of their war of independence. They firmly believe that after fighting Spain for ten years, the Spanish were completely exhausted and already defeated by the time the U.S. intervened. Journals from 1899 refer to the intervention of the U.S. Army in Cuba as "a cause of poverty and humiliation". Further, because of this intervention, they believed "the sovereignty of the Cuban people had been curtailed and violated". [1]

It is now common knowledge that the "yellow press" of William Randolph Hearst (The New York Journal) manipulated the American public into the Spanish-American War by publishing pictures of the explosion of the Maine on February 15, 1898, and headlining a rumor of Spanish sabotage. Hearst told his reporters, "You supply the photographs; I'll supply the war." In his front-page article, along with pictures of the destroyed ship, Hearst originated the slogan: "Remember the Maine".

U.S. President McKinley had sent the Maine, one of the Navy's newest vessels, to Havana harbor on a courtesy call to resume friendly port visits, but in reality, to signal American concern about Spanish intervention in Cuba. There was never any proof the Spanish had been responsible for the explosion on the Maine, and it is difficult to imagine what Spain stood to gain by destroying an American ship and killing 266 American sailors. However, the press image that the Spanish were barbarians was enough to capture the attention of the United States.

There was also an economic issue. The Spanish intervention greatly disrupted a lucrative trade, and jeopardized millions of dollars' worth of American property in Cuba. So, incited by the newspaper headline, few Americans paused to insist on proof. The rumor of Spanish sabotage was enough to launch a war.

On April 24, 1898, the U.S. declared war on Spain, and historians continue to debate whether President William McKinley led or followed public opinion into this conflict. "Nowhere among the reasons for going to war with Spain was the right of Cubans to control their own affairs given consideration by American statesmen." [2]

Further, while Americans have considered the Platt Amendment an instrument for mediating and resolving internal disputes in Cuba, Cubans have regarded it as a permit for the U.S. to intervene in Cuban affairs for its own selfish purposes. This Amendment, drawn up by the U.S. at the end of the Spanish-American War for Cuban signature, implied the U.S. would govern Cuba until the Cubans were ready to take control of their own destiny. Cubans have long felt that the Platt Amendment imposed a government on them. [3]

In 1905, Teddy Roosevelt officially gave up the United States' right of intervention, lifting restrictions on

Cuba's ability to negotiate treaties with others or borrow money from others. Then, in 1928, with the Memorandum on the Monroe Doctrine, Coolidge ended the more serious American meddling in Cuba's domestic affairs, leaving the Cuban government, as Julius Pratt reported in his paper, America's Colonial Experience, "free to develop into the type of corrupt dictatorship that was seemingly indigenous to the soil."[4]

By 1934, a reciprocal trade agreement replaced the old commercial treaty and succeeded in stimulating the Cuban Economy, but it bound Cuba even more tightly to the U.S. and made her vulnerable to unilateral changes in American Policy. During all these policy transformations, the U.S. Navy retained occupation of the land known as Guantanamo Bay.

In January of 1959, a charismatic leader by the name of Fidel Castro came to power in Cuba, and for the first time in its history, the Naval Base was confronted by a Cuban government openly hostile to the United States. Although the Cubans had in no way interfered with Guantanamo at that time (nor was there any indication that they might do so in the near future), the military authorities in command of the base made the decision in October of 1959 not to allow any U.S. personnel to enter Cuba proper. This action was taken to preclude even the slightest excuse for Castro's Revolutionary Government to take offense.

In March 1960, a French ship, the La Coubre exploded while unloading munitions in Havana harbor, causing heavy casualties. Fidel Castro immediately called it sabotage and blamed the United States. This was a turning point in U.S.-Cuban relations, as Castro shed any pretense of accommodation. It was then he delivered his defiant anti-American speech, ending with what would become the most sacred slogan of the

17

Cuban Revolution: "patria o muerte" - *fatherland or death*!

By late 1960, the United States had enacted an embargo that prohibited the export of most goods to Cuba. Not surprisingly, in January of 1961, a formal break in diplomatic relations between U.S. and Cuba occurred, and Castro's Revolutionary government prohibited informal entry of Cubans onto the Base, which meant the gate leading from Cuba became more heavily secured. Previously, Cubans seeking employment could pass freely between Cuba proper and the land leased by the U.S. Even under these restrictions, Base activities continued without serious disruption.

Concurrently with all these events, from early 1960, Castro's forces had been fighting only slightly veiled CIA-instigated saber-rattling. These activities included operatives running back and forth between Cuba and Florida, blowing up factories, staging hit-and-run attacks against the Cuban coast, buzzing Cuban air fields, and flying high-altitude reconnaissance missions over the island. The most blatant of these intimidations was the staging of an exercise called PHIBRIGLEX-62, in which Marines invaded the mythical Republic of Vieques to unseat an invented dictator called "Ortsac". . . Castro spelled backward. [5]

In this climate, during April 1961, Cuban forces loyal to and led by Castro, overwhelmed a CIA-backed invasion of Cuban exiles at the Bay of Pigs in south-central Cuba. This demonstrated that more would be needed than a minor invasion by poorly trained and lightly armed Cuban exiles to topple Castro. It would take a direct invasion by the Americans. From the Cuban perspective, therefore, no one doubted **whether** the blow would come from the U.S.; the only question was **when**. "Had there been no Bay of Pigs invasion, or had the invasion been a success instead of a humiliation, the world may never have faced the terrible events that were to follow."[6] So, by the time the actual Cuban Missile Crisis erupted on October 22, 1962, Cuba had been preparing for battle, materially and psychologically, for nineteen months. The atmosphere was rife with feelings of fear, resentment, and hostility, periodically whipped up by Castro's long harangues. On assuming power in 1959, he delivered a seven-hour speech, which some claim must be a world record for speech-making.

Between August and October of 1962, while we were settling into our idyllic life at Gitmo, the Cuban revolutionary leadership was traveling to the USSR to negotiate a military agreement for a large movement of Soviet troops and materiel to Cuba. Castro firmly believed this action was not only required to protect his country against a larger more powerful one, but he had convinced himself it was absolutely within the principles of international law. Even so, Castro had suggested making it public that Russia was deploying nuclear-tipped missiles into Cuba. He continued to receive assurances from the Soviets that the nuclear weapons were for defensive reasons. Andre Gromyko, the United States foreign minister of the Soviet Union in 1962 has been quoted as saying, "This action was intended to strengthen the defensive capability of Cuba. To avert the threats against it. I repeat, to strengthen the defensive capability of Cuba. That is all."[7].

Hence, the secret and blatant accumulation of forces and equipment on Cuban soil. Castro implicitly trusted the Russian leadership. He looked up to them as being more aware of the global situation than was he. Thus firmly convinced that he was within the dictates of international law, Castro worked feverishly, with Soviet assistance, to secretly build a fortress against the massive assault he believed the Bay of Pigs foreshadowed. And, even as the Soviet reinforcements of men and materials arrived, Castro was convinced that the entity ultimately protecting Cuba against an all-out American invasion was the global strategic might of the USSR, not the rockets.

In the aftermath of this secret deployment, historians have questioned Castro's sanity. Castro was not insane in 1962; he was merely misled.

Not only Castro, but his followers in the Revolutionary movement, inflamed with over a decade of righteous indignation, were fully convinced that the security of their nation was at risk. They were prepared to fight to the death in the event of an enemy invasion of their country. The fighting spirit of the Soviet troops transported to Cuba was equally as high. They felt honor-bound to defend the island of Cuba from attack against a larger and more powerful country. Both Cuban and Soviet forces were ready and willing to fight to the very last man to defend the interests of Revolutionary Cuba. "They had nowhere to withdraw. No retreat was possible." [8]

A brief Reuters News Agency item on October 21, 1962 reported:
The Cuban Armed Forces Ministry Sunday claimed United States troops at the Guantanamo Base Saturday night fired three shots into Cuban territory 'endangering the lives of our men.' It was the 188th denunciation by the government of Fidel Castro of United States 'provocations'. [9]

By the time of the crisis, the U.S.S.R. had transferred 43,000 men to this small island in the Caribbean only

90 miles and eight jet minutes from the mainland of the U.S. [10] Never before in the history of the Soviet Armed Forces or in the history of Russia had so many troops been transported to the other side of the ocean. Day and night was devoted to these preparations, all of which were done in absolute secrecy. Khrushchev advised, "Do not rush. Do everything in such a way that U.S public opinion will not be aware of this until November 4." [11]

Castro was a product of a history the United States and Cuba shared but understood very differently. He conceived his mission was to defend the sovereignty of Cuba; nothing was as central to the character of Cuban nationality as his notion of struggle for self-determination and sovereignty. "This chronicle of resentment, misinformation, miscalculation, and misperception culminated in the Cuban Missile Crisis of October 1962. Ignorance of the backlog of historic Cuban grievance blinded the U.S. to the reality that it was challenging the revolution at its strongest point – the point at which the past and present converged in the defense of *patria*." [12]

Furthermore, there were tremendous insufficiencies in the U.S. intelligence gathering. In early October of 1962, American intelligence estimated there were 10,000 Soviet military personnel in Cuba. By the middle of November, the estimate was increased to 16,000, and even in 1963, this final estimate was mistakenly thought to be about 22,000. The actual number was 43,000, along with 270,000 well-armed Cuban troops. And both forces, in the words of their commanders, were determined to "fight to the death". [13]

In hindsight, this is a prime example of how a war can arise between two countries when even the leaders don't know what's going on. The fact that the actual total of Soviet troop involvement was underestimated *by half,* and more importantly, that the U.S. did not even realize these were Soviet <u>combat</u> forces, most certainly helped prevent the crisis from becoming sharper than it was.

And we on the Naval Base, in the very epicenter of this action, knew even less. The Marine Barracks Intelligence Officer, Captain William R. Gentry, had come to our back door on October 17, 1962, asking to borrow our Time magazine so he could "try to find out what was going on". Thus did we continue our everyday lives, totally unaware that behind Guantanamo was the sea and on the other three sides was Communist Cuba.

[1] James G. Blight, Bruce J. Allyn, & David A. Welch – <u>Cuba on the Brink</u> - Pantheon Books, NY – 1993, 165
[2] Blight, etc. Ibid, 331
[3] Blight, etc. Ibid, 43
[4] Blight, etc. Ibid, 333
[5] Blight, etc. Ibid, 338
[6] Jennings, Peter and Brewster, Todd – <u>The Century</u> – Doubleday (NY, London, Sydney, Toronto, Auckland) 2000, 373
[7] Blight, etc. Ibid, 41
[8] Blight, etc. Ibid, 62
[9] The Salt Lake Tribune, Salt Lake City, Utah – Monday – October 22, 1962
[10] Peter Wyden, <u>Bay of Pigs, The Untold Story</u>, Simon and Schuster, NY – 1979, 66.
[11] James G. Blight, Bruce J. Allyn, & David A. Welch – <u>Cuba on the Brink</u>, Pantheon Books, NY – 1993, 79.
[12] Blight, etc. Ibid, 16-17
[13] Blight, etc. Ibid, 40

4

Paradox in Paradise

The same attributes that made Guantanamo such an ideal training base translated into nearly perfect weather conditions for military dependents, and within a few weeks, the children and I became fully entrenched in this tropical paradise. Temperatures were consistently comfortable and the sun graced us daily in a cloudless sky. Compared with most cities in the United States, the Gitmo lifestyle would have seemed like an endless vacation, but in spite of all this, for those of us trying to maintain a household, it presented a unique set of circumstances.

For example, there wasn't a grocery store on every corner competing for our business. Food was available for sale in only one place . . . the Base Commissary. One day I arrived at the produce section only to be confronted with 21 nearly empty bins. After inquiry, I was informed the 'fruit ship' only arrived every other week, this being the second Monday before 'fruit ship' Thursday.

As I was trying to decide what I would substitute for salad the rest of the week, a woman walked deliberately past the wilted mess and asked an employee when he was going to put out the new lettuce. He told her this was the new lettuce and there would be no more until the fruit ship arrived, unless someone wanted to swim to Norfolk for it.

Our challenges were not restricted to food. Instead of a selection of department and specialty stores tempting us with an infinite array of merchandise, we had only the Post Exchange (known as the PX). It served as a

23

combination department store, variety store, and drug store, leaving much to be desired in all categories. For hardware-related items, there was the General Store.

A particular frustration was the arrival of toys only **once** a year. It was essential to make selections early and often, because after they were gone, there would be no more toys until the following August. Armed with this bit of information, every trip I made to the PX included the purchase of at least one toy, which I'd toss up into our attic. Early in October of 1962, improvising something on which to climb, I took inventory. My purchases included (in part) 29 coloring books, 7 trucks, 9 dolls, 3 different types of trains, and a handy-dandy, mechanical bartender who emitted smoke from his ears.

My worst obsession, however, was light bulbs. When we first arrived, nothing was available but 40-watt bulbs. Soon thereafter, even these were gone. Two rooms had to be closed off entirely, because we'd stolen bulbs to keep the rest of the house illuminated. As soon as the new supply of light bulbs arrived, I went out of control, and accumulated a stockpile to rival the General Store.

We won't even talk about shoes!

Shortly after my arrival, I became aware of an undercurrent of resentment among many of the Cubans employed on the base, the reasons for which escaped me at the time. It was especially noticeable during visits to the one and only gas station. The Cubans employed there were often surly and unaccommodating, but we either bought our gas there or went without.

After several occasions of indifferent treatment at the gas station, my initial encounter with the attendant at the first pump on the left was a complete surprise. I was greeted like a valued customer of long-standing with an exuberant, "Buenas dias, Senora!" after which he began to vigorously clean my windows without even being asked.

Herberto (their names were embroidered on their pockets) was not satisfied with a simple salutation. From there, he inquired about my health, and when I could not respond in his native tongue, he very patiently gave me a lesson in Spanish, whether I wanted it or not.

In the future, I made it a point to wait in line, if necessary, to buy my gas from Herberto. And, because of him, I vowed to learn at least enough Spanish to return his greetings in kind. His delight with each new word kept this interest alive. It was my first real reminder that we were living in a foreign country.

Base life certainly presented its challenges, some with definitely frustrating overtones. Looking back now, however, I distinctly recall that the time spent with Herberto, an unofficial ambassador for his country, affected me deeply. He portrayed the dignity and pride of doing the job given him to the best of his ability. He acted as if every encounter was the most important one of the day to him. In view of the activities going on in his country (of which I was unaware at the time), I now have the feeling he was never certain what his future might be, but his attitude reflected a determination to make each day, lived well, sufficient unto itself.

5

The Beach

Once a week, I would ignore the dust on the floors, load Colleen and Billy into the car, and spend the morning at Kittery Beach. Nothing was very distant on this 45-square mile Base and the trip to the beach only took us about 20 minutes. On weekends, crowds converged, but during the week, we had this haven to ourselves.

Kittery Beach had been created by the SeaBees (Navy Mobile Construction Battalion) about 1954. Several cabanas had been constructed, equipped with tables and benches. The SeaBees had blasted a large area out of the coral to make it conducive to swimming. This pool-like area, with graduated depth, was surrounded by a natural coral reef. It never ceased to amaze me the way the water magically changed colors as the depth and density altered. Protected from any large waves by the coral enclosure, the children could float in their tubes rather freely.

Often small tropical fish would make their way over the coral wall and share our swimming space. The most common were yellow with black flecks, black with a red stripe, and aqua blue with white stripes. They would just flit within our view and flit away, but it was a constant source of delight when we spotted one. It seemed like a small miracle to have such a retreat so accessible. The water washed away any tension and the brisk breeze tossed worries to the wind, and best of all, I could not see the dust on the floors waiting to be mopped.

Ironically, Kittery Beach represented another of those Gitmo paradoxes. While it was a place for peaceful relaxation, encouraged by the rhythmic lapping of gentle waves against the shore, high on a cliff overlooking this idyllic scene were the soldiers of Castro's Revolutionary forces, the hard metal barrels of their rifles glinting in the sunlight. They were guarding what came to be known as the 'cactus curtain'. It was one of the perimeters between the Naval Base and Castro's Cuba. Before being guarded, there were Cubans desperate enough for freedom to climb down the cliff of coral rock and take their chances swimming across the narrow channel that separated the Base from Cuba proper.

Although the forces guarding this perimeter never attempted to initiate any contact with us, it seemed only neighborly to me to acknowledge their presence. So, after we were settled in our cabana, and the children were happily occupied with shovels and buckets, I would usually look up, shielding my eyes against the sun, and wave at them. They would respond in kind, with just a short wave, and a tip of their hats. This simple gesture seemed to establish a rapport that made coexistence during our time together at least more comfortable for me. And, I felt somewhat certain our presence for those few hours a week, and the activities of the children, probably relieved the boredom of their lonely vigil.

An additional attraction at Kittery Beach was a large iguana. He seemed to get used to us after awhile and know we intended him no harm. He would crawl from behind the rocks and take a sunbath near our cabana, his hind legs sprawled out like a dog in utter laziness and nonchalance.

Iguana, I learned from research, are a remnant of prehistoric times, and the number of such reptiles in our world is diminishing. These large and powerful lizards sometimes reach a length of six feet, but the one who frequented Kittery Beach was much smaller.

Our companion (and who knew if it was the same iguana every visit) did not hesitate to crawl closer when I would throw him a piece of carrot or apple core. He would then incline his head toward me in an almost gentle or coy manner before retrieving the morsel from the ground. After capture, Iguanas recognizing kind treatment, can become very tame. They have been known to rush to meet the person who feeds them, unhesitatingly taking food from the fingers. But since adult lizards are vicious fighters, dealing hard blows with their tails while employing both teeth and claws if restrained, I did not push our relationship to this extent.

Sun, surf, exotic fish, a nearly extinct visitor, and of course, the guardians on the cliff above were the ingredients for a most unusual outing. Regardless of other commitments, I made it a point to keep this weekly date at Kittery Beach because I somehow knew that nowhere else in life would I ever encounter a place quite like it.

5-1 Swim area of Kittery Beach enclosed by coral wall

5-2 Castro's militiamen (at arrow) guarding on the cliff above Kittery Beach

6

Tibbs

About a month after our arrival, my neighbor, Claire Seibert, asked if I might be interested in buying a horse. She suggested the naked ambience of this place we were calling home, the flora and fauna that was the essence of Cuba, was really only available aboard a horse. A short ride into the foothills afforded a glimpse of this foreign country without the military trappings the U.S. Government had imposed when they converted this corner of the country into a Naval Base.

Knowledge of a horse for sale at the Family Corral was usually passed by word of mouth. Claire told me about the availability of a seven-year-old roan gelding with a white diamond on his forehead. Tibbs was not very large . . . just under 14 hands, and a perfect size for my entry into the equestrian world.

Even though I'd never owned a horse and my only experience with them was at riding stables, Claire promised to show me the ropes (literally and figuratively). The corral bill for stabling and feeding a horse was $15 per month. I recognized this as another of those once-in-a-lifetime opportunities, and for an exchange of very little money, Tibbs became mine.

As a new owner, I was directed to a locker in the tack room containing the "dowry" of my animal. It included a horse brush, a rope, a screwdriver, and a few lacy cobwebs. Claire graciously showed me what to do with all this paraphernalia, since she hailed from Texas and had grown up with horses.

The screwdriver puzzled me. Claire grabbed her screwdriver and demonstrated how to clean manure and rocks out of Tibbs' hoofs. She just tapped him near the hoof and he bent his knee and picked up his hoof for her. She balanced it on her knee and proceeded to dig and scrape. When she next showed me how to look for ticks in his ears, I wondered what I'd let myself in for. But I soon realized these chores were a small price to pay for encountering fields of giant cacti in full bloom or meandering through grass that hid all but the horse's neck. As we'd sail by the Base golf course, Claire would often say, "Remind me to take up golf some day!"

None of these Cuban horses was for inexperienced riders. They were exciting mounts who knew the trails better than their riders and were not hesitant to take advantage if the rider did not have proper control. I soon learned a firm grip on the reigns gave Tibbs a sense that someone was in charge. His bolting about like a teenager stemmed mostly from insecurity, not malice. I also learned he would 'spook' at anything white such as an old paper towel on the trail or a white blossom on a bush. I came to realize these sudden sideways jerks were caused by his fear, not any desire to unseat me. After a few trips, we developed a comfortable rapport and he stopped fighting me and rather seemed to enjoy the outings as much as I did.

Along with Claire, two other women, Chick, (the wife of Marine Colonel George W. Killen, Commander of the Gitmo Marine Barracks), and Helen, (the wife of Public Works Corps employee, Robert H. Work) were already deeply entrenched in a delightful routine which they invited me to share. Once a week, we would leave the stable about 9 a.m., ride to Kittery Beach, and have a swim and some lunch before riding back again. The round-trip on horseback was about 17 miles.

While on the trail, Helen Work would often tell us about life in Gitmo 'before Castro'. She and her husband, Bob, were almost Base legends. They had come to Gitmo from their native state of Colorado eight years before. During that time, Bob had been a civilian worker employed by the Public Works Corps, and Helen had served as a volunteer Girl Scout leader. When Helen first arrived (1954), there were no complaints about lack of styles or sizes in women's clothing, as there were none available. The tour for civilians was 18 months (Bob had extended his tour several times), and those coming were told in advance to bring enough women's and children's clothing for their entire tour of duty. Any additional needs would have to be ordered from catalogs.

The 'closing of the gate', when Castro had ordered searches and passes, had been a difficult adjustment for the Work family. It had meant a whole change of lifestyle. In previous years, they had developed friendships with many Cuban Nationals. A three-day weekend often included a drive to Havana to visit one of them. Parties were never held on base. There were Cuban-style beach events with roast pig and all the trimmings, or more formal affairs at a night club on Brooks Island, not far from the Base.

On other interesting trips to Manzanillo, and Cienfuegos, the Work family would visit with acquaintances who were farmers. These friendly, generous people would present the family with the cream of their crops before sending them home. Helen told us with obvious relish about how much richer Scouting had been when the Cuban and the Base scouts could combine for special events and march in parades together, carrying the Cuban and American flags side by side. "It's so sad," she said, "that the current situation has changed all that." We, who had never experienced the advantage of open exchange with our host country, were not aware of how much we had missed.

It was 91 degrees on October 17, 1962 when Chick, Helen, Claire and I set out for our regular Wednesday ride to Kittery Beach. After arrival, we were unrolling our squashed sandwiches from the saddle bags, when our attention was drawn by the reflection of glinting metal from the neighboring cliff. As we turned to exchange our customary wave with the Cuban guards, we couldn't help but notice some glaring differences. We saw five guards and we'd never seen more than two previously. Three of these guards had climbed up a tree, and were waving a white cloth and yelling something. This was a complete departure from the norm. None of the guards on previous occasions had ever tried to call out to us. This, and the increase in numbers, weren't the only changes. The three guards up in the tree had on different colored uniforms and different shaped hats than we'd ever seen before.

Friday evening of that week, October 19, 1962, the siren sounded, alerting us to the beginning of another Naval Emergency Ground Defense Exercise (DefEx). These drills required Military personnel to spend the weekend in defensive positions. They had been a regular feature of the Base training schedule for the past two years. No one was alarmed by the prospect of yet another one. For we Marine wives, it only meant we would not be seeing our husbands that weekend.

I did not know it then, but this particular weekend marked the beginning of the most extensive DefEx ever conducted at Guantanamo Bay. For 36 hours, the Sailors, Marines, and SeaBees of the emergency defense forces were the **only** troops available to defend the Base. In an article about it in an issue of Leatherneck Magazine, a SeaBee reported when he was told he could have all the ammunition he wanted instead of having it carefully counted out, he knew things might get serious. He said he and his comrades-in-arms were in those defensive positions for two days before the Marines landed. In the article, he is quoted as saying, "When the transport planes started landing at Leeward Point and the Marines came streaming out, I never felt better in my life." [1]

---

[1] Leatherneck – Magazine of the Marines – February 1963 in an article by SSgt Charles Kester, 31.

6-1 Author aboard Tibbs

6-2 Others in the Wednesday Morning Riding Club – from left: Claire Seibert, Helen Work, Chick Killen almost lost in the tall Cuban grass on the horse trail to the beach

7

Not Your Usual Weekend

On Saturday, October 20, 1962, I decided to take Billy and Colleen to the Officer's Club pool. We spent most of the day there, enjoying the idyllic weather in the company of other wives and children whose husbands and fathers were also participating in the DefEx.

As usual, I brought a camera. We were accustomed to ships anchored in the Bay off the Officer's Club, so it didn't surprise me when I saw yet another one, although this ship was rather larger than most. When developed, the candid snapshots I took that day revealed the nuclear aircraft carrier *Enterprise* anchored in the Bay beyond the Officer's Club.

On this particular Saturday, after our return from the pool, some of the Marine wives congregated in the driveway shared by our family and the Seibert's. Claire suggested some lemonade. As we were sipping our lemonade, Claire brought out a jig-saw puzzle and dumped it onto the large dining room table. She began sorting nonchalantly through the pile for straight edges. The rest of us gravitated over. We visited as the perimeter of the puzzle came together. It was a pleasant communal diversion. Mickey, wife of Captain Gerald Hagen, was the first to leave for dinner preparations; then the rest of us wandered back to our separate homes, with the understanding that we would return to keep each other company over the puzzle as soon as young ones were safely tucked into bed.

While working on the puzzle that night, I heard the cry of my youngest float across the still air. Once asleep, my two rarely awakened. I rushed across the driveway to my backdoor, and into Billy's bedroom. Heat emanated from his body as I lifted him from the bed. I knew even without checking that he had a substantial fever.

Without even stopping to check how high his fever might be, I carried him next door. His cries had not abated. The other wives confirmed my opinion, and decided he needed some immediate medical attention. This was no trivial decision, because there was a strict curfew and blackout on the base for the entire duration of a DefEx, but armed with communal consent, I bundled Billy into our car for the short drive to the hospital. The other wives would, of course, be attentive to my daughter should she need anything while I was gone.

Even though I used the car's low beams, my headlights seemed like searchlights in the otherwise black night. I do remember the mixed emotions my husband reported when he told me later about the announcement in Command Headquarters that an unidentified 1960 Blue Ford Skylark was proceding along Sherman Avenue at a high rate of speed. I was eager to get this illicit trip over as quickly as possible.

The doctor on duty said it was no wonder Billy was crying. He had two terribly inflamed eardrums from an obvious ear infection. He was given a penicillin shot, and I was sent home with liquid penicillin in a pink suspension. I would be giving this medicine to him four times a day for the next two weeks. These weeks encompassed our sudden 'evacuation' from Gitmo by ship. After this trip, every piece of clothing Billy owned was stained with this bright pink liquid, a result of either the ship or Billy's stomach lurching.

The next morning, I was awakened with an unfamiliar low rumbling. Something seemed wrong! With a vague sense of discomfort, I thrashed in the bed. Still partially asleep, I opened my eyes and saw sunlight filtering through the wooden louvers of my bedroom window, so I knew the incessant rumbling wasn't part of a dream.

For some unknown reason, I was filled with apprehension. The ambience was charged with something I couldn't identify. Although it was comfortably warm, goose pimples began forming on the back of my arms. I was as frightened as if it was pitch black in the middle of the night and I had heard someone trying to break into the house.

To relieve my fear, I flung off the light bedding, hit the ground running, and followed the noise. As I ran through the house and unlocked the back door, the rumbling increased, confirming my initial impression that it was coming from outside. Still in my nightgown and bare feet, I ran outside, looking in all directions. The unusual noise drowned out the gentle call of the morning dove. In fact, it effectively drowned out every other sound. Looking around, I could see nothing to indicate what was causing this rumbling vibration, yet it enveloped me.

Finally, I looked up. My view of the sky was obscured by the dense leaves of the mango tree, so I ran past the clothes lines and around the mango tree to get a clearer view. Directly overhead, I located the source of the low rumble. As a Marine wife, I recognized a C-130 jet transport passing overhead. Shielding my eyes against the rising sun, I watched as the landing gear of the aircraft slowly lowered, giving it the appearance of a giant mosquito. The jet's destination was obviously McCalla Field Naval Air Station, across Guantanamo

Bay from our home. I waited and watched as it emitted its scream and landed.

As the furor of the landing died down, I heard from behind me a continuation of the low rumbling, this time from a greater distance. While I pursued my search of the skies, the noise grew closer. Then above me, through the palm leaves, yet another C-130 nosed into view.

I ran next door and began pounding on Claire's door. She emerged, also in nightgown and bare feet. Since the sound of the aircraft drowned out conversation, I just grabbed her hand and pulled her out into the middle of our adjoining yards and motioned upward. The shrill parade continued, as another C-130 streaked above us, preparing to land.

By then, Claire's teenage daughters, Kay and Beth, had joined us, and all we could do was look at each other and gesture, because nothing could be heard except the jet transports vaulting overhead. Glancing at my watch, I noticed it was only 6:15 on this Sunday morning of October 21, 1962.

The steady, low rumbling and vibration continued past noon. I thought it was the result of a sky that remained thick with the arrival of aircraft. What I didn't know was that all night and into the day, truckloads of Marines, jeeps with recoilless cannon, tanks, and other heavy vehicles were also arriving on the Base. There was something soul-shaking about the noise and vibration of heavy tanks. The very earth trembles and quivers.

The pot-bellied Hercules transports that droned over my back yard each carried men of an alert battalion of the 2nd Marine Divison. Their 92 red canvas bucket seats had been loaded very early that morning at

Camp Lejeune, North Carolina with Marines in full battle dress. Meanwhile, President John F. Kennedy was charting a course that would be marked boldly in the annals of history. Washington and civilian agencies were on a status of "def-con" (defense condition), which meant skeleton staffs were stationed at undisclosed places out of the District of Columbia to be able to run the Government after any attack. The capitol's Cathedral school staked out an air raid shelter for its children under the tomb of Woodrow Wilson. Children in Los Angeles, California crouched in a school corridor in preparation for a nuclear attack, shielding the backs of their necks with their hands.

Why all these preparations? A Russian military base had been erected in Cuba with alarming speed and effrontery. It had become transformed into a base for mid-range (1200-mile) missiles. Thirty of them were set up in Cuba. The Russian President, Nikita Khrushchev, did not even seem to care whether he was caught in the act. Camouflage was minimal, and the Russians had cleared away large areas around the military posts to prevent brush fires from rocket blasts. These scars on the ground were clearly visible. Air, reconnaissance photos taken by U-2 aircraft made it clear to the Defense Department that nearly every point from Lima, Peru to Hudson Bay in Canada would lie within push-button range of thermonuclear bombs in Cuba.

This attempted military coup would go down in history as a miscalculation of the American spirit and will on the part of President Khrushchev. Our peaceful residential community was transformed overnight from suburbia into a bristling fortress. Over three hundred officers and three thousand men of the Navy, Marines, and SeaBees converted it into a ring of steel, facing Fidel Castro's forces on three sides, and ready for any eventuality. The steel perimeter clamped around Guantanamo by the United States could have been the trip-wire for WWIII, but only if Khrushchev chose to make it so.

Not only in the nation's capitol, but also among our little community in Gitmo, there was an unbearable sense of foreboding and tension. Luckily, we who were gathered around the table on that lovely Saturday evening in October of 1962 were unaware of the transformation that had taken place in Cuba. Had we been, working on a simple jigsaw puzzle would certainly not have been enough to distract us.

7-1 A large ship in the Bay near the Officers' Club, later
    identified as the nuclear aircraft carrier, *Enterprise*

7-2 Lots of activity in Guantanamo Bay one Sunday
    morning in October 1962, as seen from author's
    backyard

8

Evolution of a Crisis

Long before our rude awakening at the Guantanamo Bay Naval Base on Sunday morning, October 21, 1962, the worldwide nuclear drama began to manifest itself and gradually build in intensity. Surveillance and evaluation by Joint Photo Interpretation Units pouring over thousands of reconnaissance pictures of Cuba left no doubt that the Soviets had installed mobile missiles that could easily hit targets on the East Coast, and were also preparing sites for 2,500-mile missiles that could destroy cities in all but the northwestern corner of the United States. There was unmistakable evidence that Khrushchev had a gun directed at America's belly.

The information in this chapter was gleaned from Life and Look magazine articles published in December 1962.[1] During October of 1962, none of this unfolding drama was common knowledge at Gitmo.

Robert S. McNamara, Secretary of Defense, had called an emergency session of the Joint Chiefs of Staff on October 15, but decided not to bother the President until they had all the facts at hand. On that same date, the CIA went into emergency session. Why? On a reconnaissance mission that day, photos from U-2 planes had disclosed eight ballistic launchpads in Cuba of Soviet mid-range missiles. It was a terrifying discovery. For thirteen days, the world sat dumbstruck from the possibility of imminent nuclear destruction.

After nightfall, McNamara had made the decision to inform the State Department. Secretary of State, Dean Rusk, was alerted, and Deputy Under Secretary, Alexis Johnson was called. Top State officials attended a midnight meeting. The hour was late and it was decided to wait until morning to inform the President.

Early on Tuesday, October 16, President Kennedy was advised that U-2 planes and low-flying fighters had returned with photographic evidence that the Russians were cramming the 750-mile-long Caribbean Island of Cuba with light jet bombers and missiles that pointed at America's heartland. President Kennedy took this news calmly, but quickly ordered stepped-up aerial reconnaissance. He set an urgent meeting of key counselors for 11:45 am, where the CIA and two photo evaluators showed the incriminating pictures. This group assumed the formal title of 'Executive Committee of the National Security Council', and presented options to the President. No decision was made at this time.

In a continuation of this drama, the Executive Committee met again on Wednesday, October 17, at which time a surprise invasion of Cuba was eliminated as a course of action. Coincidentally, a Gallup Poll in the Washington Post of that day revealed that 51 percent of the American people thought an invasion of Cuba would provoke all-out war with Russia, while 37 percent thought not. At this time, the undisclosed opinion of the Executive Committee was that if all other measures failed, an invasion might be necessary.

On the surface, Washington social life proceeded normally. Jacqueline Kennedy received a citation for raising the cultural standards of the nation. The President was given a red-velvet Arabian saddle by the Crown Prince of Libya.

Meanwhile, around the nation, small but critical steps were taken. A Navy cargo plane landed in Rochester, New York to pick up extra film-processing equipment, and took it back to the Naval Air Station at Jacksonville, Florida. This equipment was needed for the river of pictures coming from planes photographing Cuba. A worldwide alert put all U.S. forces on guard. Second-level officers were informed of worries over the presence of 11-28 bombers in Cuba. The missile-site discovery was still a closely held secret.

By prearrangement, the President and Vice President kept campaign speaking dates. McNamara strode into his office on Thursday, October 18 at 7:10 a.m. and soon the Big Three aides of the crisis week (McNamara, Robert Kennedy and General Maxwell Taylor) were in a huddle. New photos indicated more missile bases were under construction, giving an urgency to the meetings. The Executive Committee began to talk seriously about a blockade. John T. McNaughton, Defense general counsel, was brought in to confer about the legal questions involved in such a move. A bevy of Navy lawyers joined the deliberations

Long-planned amphibious war games off Puerto Rico, called Phibriglex-62, provided a mask for the growing movement of troops and ships. More than 6,000 Marines, moving East from California in 40 warships, were planning to converge in the Caribbean for these war games, and a special air strike force was poised to fly into position. Florida fairly bristled with arms.

The Executive Committee met continuously. They were actually meeting in session on the floor below where Dean Rusk was entertaining Soviet Foreign Minister Andrei A. Gromyko at dinner. At 9 p.m. on October 18, the group had to move to the White House. To avoid arousing talk with a cavalcade of cars, ten men piled in George Ball's car. Robert Kennedy sat on the knees of Alexis Johnson. One occupant said, "My God, suppose we're all in an accident? What will the papers say?" [2]

In an earlier meeting, Kennedy and Rusk, talked with Gromyko. Kennedy made no mention of the Cuban missile sites. He had no intention of tipping his hand to the Russians until American policy jelled. During the meeting, Kennedy left the room and returned to read sternly from a statement he had made dated September 13, 1962. This statement vowed to do, "whatever must be done if the Soviet buildup turned Cuba into an offensive military base threatening our security". [3] Gromyko blandly replied that the arms in Cuba were purely defensive in nature. This lie seemed especially offensive to Kennedy considering recent evidence to the contrary.

Another lie became temporary Pentagon policy. On Friday, October 19, rumors of a U.S military build-up reached the Pentagon pressroom. Queries were put to Assistant Secretary of Defense, Arthur Sylvester. The Pentagon issued the following statement:

A Pentagon spokesman denied tonight that any alert has been ordered or that any emergency military measures have been set in motion against Communist-ruled Cuba. Further, the spokesman said, the Pentagon has no information indicating the presence of offensive weapons in Cuba.

Prior to this, Rear Admiral George Burkley, assistant White House physician, had informed the President he was suffering from a slight cold. Even so, at 11 a.m. October 19, President Kennedy flew west for a pre-arranged campaign trip. The President's medical condition was eventually used to good advantage. A 7 p.m. phone call from the White House revealed that more hard-photo intelligence had arrived and a courier would fly this new photo evidence out West.

"How hairy is it?" O'Donnell asked on the phone.

"Pretty hairy. So bad I think he ought to come home."

By Saturday, October 20, the President's cold had worsened, and he had a valid excuse to cancel the rest of his trip. O 'Donnell phoned D.C. "Don't send a courier. We're coming home". Of this cancelled trip, some punsters remarked, "This cover story has a germ of truth in it." [4]

The count-down accelerated as Kennedy arrived by helicopter on the south lawn of the White House at 1:37 pm. October 20. By 2:30, he had assembled a meeting in the Oval Office. The decision was made that a blockade, combined with a demand to Russia and an appeal to the U.S. Security Council, would be the U.S. course of action. As part of the invasion plan, President Kennedy and Cabinet and top military and civilian leaders would repair to secret, atom-proof shelters in the mountains of Virginia and Maryland, because if any gunfire was exchanged, no one could foretell with certainty the Kremlin's response.

The Pentagon, normally deserted on Saturday, was alive with comings and goings. The legal quarantine proclamation was finalized by Abram Chayes, State Department legal adviser. Lights burned late. Bundy and Rusk labored over the speech the President intended to make to the nation, now in its seventh draft.

More than four thousand air miles away, Vice President Johnson caught a plane for D.C. Around the country, personnel were alerted to assemble in the Nation's Capitol. Livingston Merchanat, retired diplomat, was summoned away from the Princteon-Colgate football game. The CIA briefed Dwight D. Eisenhower, who had been flown from Gettysburg in a helicopter to D.C.

Security became a problem as the media, doing their job, took notice of the unusual activities. It was decided that 15 members of the Press Corps should leave to cover the amphibious exercises previously scheduled in Puerto Rico, even though the White House had diverted these exercises.

All over D.C. on Saturday, October 20, frantic hostesses found their parties in shambles. Ranking guests failed to show, or spent time on den and kitchen phones. Behind this cover, the grim talks continued. A Naval blockade, to be called a 'quarantine', was favored by the President, in spite of advice to the contrary.

Robert Kennedy, in a pessimistic mood said, "We may all be fighting for our lives within two weeks".
5

---

[1] Life Magazine, November 2 and 9, 1962, written by Life correspondents John Dille, Military Affairs Editor, and Richard Oulahan, Jr.; Look magazine article dated December 18, 1962 by Fletcher Knebel, reporter from the Look Washington Bureau.

2 Knebel, Fletcher –Look Magazine, December 18, 1962.

3 Dille, John – Life Magazine, November 9, 1962.

4 Dille, Ibid

5 Dille, Ibid

Circles of Missile Danger

Inner Circle Shows 1,200-Mile Radius of Cuban Missile. Outer Circle Shows a 2,400-mile Radius

9

Not Your Usual Monday

It was a quiet Monday, in sharp contrast to Sunday's rude awakening. I was expecting my husband to arrive home from the DefEx, weary and disheveled from his weekend in the field, with only enough time to shower, shave, and don a clean uniform before reporting for his normal Monday duties at the Marine Barracks. And, I had a raft of questions to ask him!

While sorting the wash in the entry near the back door, I heard conversation in the driveway and went outside to see who was talking to Claire. She was in her garage pumping up a bicycle tire when Barbara, the wife of Major William McCarthy, came up the driveway. I heard Barbara say that word had been received from another Base Command that dependents would be evacuated before nightfall. Claire shrugged and said,
"I'm not going to let myself get sucked into reacting to rumors."
It did not seem plausible to me either, and what's more, I didn't want it to be true, so as I joined them, I also made light of Barbara's misgivings.

As Barbara turned to leave, she all but collided with Mickie Hagen who came running from across the street. Mickie's voice reached a crescendo as she blurted out,
"They're sending the kids home from school!"
It was about 9:30 in the morning. I didn't know what to think, but once again Claire blithely said,
"I haven't heard a word and I'm not letting myself get excited until I hear something official. Besides, I don't want to go! Come on in. Let's finish that puzzle we started last night."

We had barely settled ourselves with the puzzle when Chick Killen appeared at Claire's back door. I will never forget the look on her face. Her lips were drawn thin and taut. With effort, she seemed to force her mouth opened and requested we come into the bedroom, as Claire's maid was within ear-shot.

As Claire closed the bedroom door, I braced my back against it for support. Trying to control her trembling voice, Chick said,

"George just called. We are to be evacuated from here before five o'clock. The first bus will be here at noon. Admiral O'Donnell wants the evacuation carried out as calmly and quickly as possible."

She took a deep breath, looked fondly at each of us when she noted she had not lost us, and asked gently, "Now, will you help me pass the word to the others?"

And so we had "something official". No whistles were blown; no sound truck circulated. We walked together down our street and told the other Marine wives. This is the way the word went out in all commands. There was no hysteria, no emotional outbursts, no questions asked. There was simply *no time* for any of that!

The school children began arriving home just after 10 a.m. We were told to be ready to board buses as soon as possible. The first bus would leave at noon. We had no idea where the buses would be taking us or what to expect beyond that.

I tried vainly to stop the whirling going on inside my head. Was this real or some kind of a drill? I didn't dare not take it seriously, even though I hoped someone would appear and tell me otherwise. What to do first? I had a bare two hours to prepare myself and two toddlers for a trip of unknown duration or destination.

I scooped up the sorted wash, and dumped as much as possible into the machine. As the water ran, I tried to organize my thoughts.

In a frenzy, I rushed to the closet door on which the mimeographed evacuation instructions were posted and tore them from their taped edges. The instructions advised making these preparations ahead of time, but of course I hadn't done this.

I don't know why, but I decided the most pressing need was *"Prepare tags with sponsor's name, grade, and duty station for identification of automobile, suitcases, and small children."*

I found a package of plain 3x5 cards and sat down at the typewriter to prepare the nametags. Why didn't I hand-write them? I can type faster than I can write by hand, and I was shaking too hard to write legibly. More importantly, I needed the familiar feeling of those keys responding to my touch

Thus, I was typing, when I heard someone try my front door, which was still locked from the night before. The louvers were only partly opened, and through them I caught a glimpse of the Marine utility uniform.
"Bill", I called out!
The answer was "Yes".
Thinking with relief that it was my husband, I said, "That door's locked . . . key's in the back door."
I went charging through the house to get the key and arrived at the back door the same time as Captain Bill Hubbard, a good Marine friend from another time and place. Mixed emotions nearly undid me. It was a great surprise to see Bill Hubbard on my doorstep, and a deep disappointment to realize it was not my husband,

Bill Kendig. My forced calmness was nearly shattered. It was the closest I came to breaking down.

Bill gave me a quick hug and handed me a mimeographed message from Rear Admiral E. J. O'Donnel. It said:

"Higher authority has directed the immediate evacuation of all dependents from the Naval Base. This includes the following persons:
a. All women and children who are U.S. citizens.
b. All non-U.S. women and children whose husbands or fathers are U.S. cistizen.
c. All female employees who are U.S. citizens (except Navy Nurses)
d. All U.S. male civilian employees who desire to leave.
Please do not ask questions or request exceptions. There is no time for that. Read this notice carefully. The word will NOT be passed over WGBY [the base radio station]. DO NOT USE YOUR TELEPHONE.

*Carry out the special evacuation instructions which have already been furnished to you and which you should have posted in your home, Specifically, pick up your pre-*packed **[I was apparently not the only one who had neglected this little requirement]** *suitcases (not more than one per person). Include any special medicines, special foods, and several changes of clothes. One blanket per person may be carried. Take I.D. cards, important legal and personal papers, checkbooks, bank books, etc. Flashlights and transistor radios may be included. Tag all suitcases with your name and address. Have your two-part evacuation card filled out and ready to hand to the evacuation team when called for. Extra cards and shipping tags will be available at embarkation points. Busses will run continuously direct to the piers starting shortly after you receive this information until everyone is picked up. DO NOT PROCEED BY CAR. Leave your car at home with a tagged set of keys in the ignition or tied to the steering*

*wheel. Tie up pets in the yard. YOU MAY NOT TAKE
PETS WITH YOU. Leave house keys on table in the living
room.*

*Evacuation will be by ship. There will be plenty of food and
water and the best possible arrangements will be made for
your comfort and quick return to the United States. You
will be entirely safe. Your husbands are required for their
military duties and may not be able to see you before
departure. Friends and neighbors without small children
are requested to help those with small children in every way
both during the evacuation and aboard ship.*

*You will be given all possible assistance at the port of
debarkation. Please keep calm and carry out all directions
given you. The busses are starting their runs now. Get your
suitcases and children and wait quietly in your front yard
when ready.*

God Bless you. We will all miss you.

*PUT THIS IN YOUR PURSE. DO NOT LEAVE IT
LYING AROUND THE HOUSE OR YARD."*

*

When I had finished reading it, Bill asked if I was all
right. I briefly nodded, not trusting my voice. He then
helped me get our suitcases down from the overhead
attic, and headed toward Claire's back door.

When you leave home for an "indefinite period" (as the
President later told us), how do you begin to pack? The
restriction of one bag per person, coupled with no prior
warning, made it even more daunting. Could it possibly
be cold where we were going? Would it ever be cold
anywhere again (I was soaked with perspiration)? Did
the children even have winter clothes that would still fit
them? Of course not! At their ages, they had simply
outgrown anything they had worn last winter. We had

all been clad in tropical gear since our arrival, because average winter temperatures in Cuba were about 84 degrees. These were just some of the imponderables that ran through my mind.

I packed our bags from the dryer. Luckily I <u>had</u> a clothes dryer. One unfortunate woman had her wash already on the line and had to pack wet clothes, which were mildewed when she opened her bags on the ship.

The one thing that meant the most to me, my husband, couldn't be packed. And, there was no room for all those priceless and irreplaceable baby albums and pictures. What else really mattered?

Take one small bottle of perfume. Keep up the morale! What about diapers? Our son had been completely potty-trained for only one month. How could I expect him not to regress with change and confusion? But I didn't have <u>room</u> for diapers!

Must remember the liquid penicillin Billy had been taking for two days for his ear infection. Get the important personal papers. What about Tibbs? I located the Bill of Sale for the horse.

While I was packing, my husband came home. Neither of us lingered over our greeting, knowing it could become disastrously emotional. Although he had been one of the few Marine officers who had been in constant contact with Washington, D.C., he was under strict orders to tell me nothing! As Supply Officer, he had been informed six days previously that he would be required to furnish beds, food, and showers for an influx of thousands of new troops. He had not been given any other details, and was too busy during the DefEx making these arrangements to speculate why.

So, ignoring my questions, Bill reread the evacuation instructions to see what I might have missed. He noticed we could take one blanket each, and he prepared these, against my protests. During the whole trip, nothing made me feel more like a refugee or displaced person than that darned bedroll.

I showed Bill the stack of library books that needed returning, and shoved the Bill of Sale for the horse into his hand. He assured me that he, being the Supply Officer, would be "the man in the rear with the gear". But what do you say . . . what can you say . . . when in the back of your mind is that disquieting fear . . .although never mentioned. . . never even consciously acknowledged . . . that you might never see each other again!

Bill did what he could to help me pack, gave each of his children a quick hug, gave me a firm hand clasp and a warning look not to make the "goodbye" any more fervent, strode quickly to his jeep and drove away, never looking back. It was best . . . I knew it was best, but I watched until the jeep was out of sight.

I fed the children an early lunch of leftover fried chicken. It was getting near zero hour and I hadn't finished packing. I had to take everything out of one suitcase and begin again when it became obvious that I'd have to pack necessities first and then see if there was room for anything else. Luckily, we had a reprieve because we were on the last bus to leave our area. It was just after 1:00 p.m. when Bill Hubbard came back requesting our suitcases. At that instant, I was standing on the kitchen counter reaching into the overhead attic where I had stored all those toys. Bill helped me grab down a sailor-boy doll for Billy and a doll in her carrying case for Colleen. These dolls proved a Godsend on the ship. Bill took the suitcases, and with one child by each hand, I followed him out.

As we reached the back door, I stopped for one final look around the home I had come to love so dearly. As I passed our car in the driveway, I tied the keys onto the steering wheel, as instructed. I wondered who would find the keys and take care of the car, because who had time to worry about material things at a time like this.

During our brief wait for the bus in Chick's yard, she noticed my son's fair skin begin to turn red from the intensity of the mid-day sun. She rushed back into her house and came out with a wide-brimmed straw hat, which she plunked on Billy's head. He was too hot and uncomfortable to protest. That hat showed up thousands of miles later on his mother's head in a UP wire photo published nationally.

We boarded the bus, the last bus to leave our area. About half an hour later, we arrived at Pier Victor. It was not until then that a pier official boarded the bus and told us we would be departing on the *Upshur*, one of the fleet of Military Sea Transportation Service ships, and would disembark three days later in Norfolk, Virginia.

Although none of us on the bus that hot October day knew it, we were living history. The United States was in the middle of a Missile Crisis and we, the dependents of the United States Naval Base in Guantanamo Bay, Cuba, were President Kennedy's last impediment to action. With us gone, he would be free to call Khrushchev's bluff!

9-1 Make-shift identification tags author prepared to hang around her children's necks

URGENT

TO ALL BASE RESIDENTS

Higher authority has directed the immediate evacuation of all dependents from the Naval Base. This includes the following persons:

a. All women and children who are U. S. citizens.
b. All non-U.S. women and children whose husbands or fathers are U. S. citizens.
c. All female employees who are U. S. citizens (except Navy Nurses).
d. All U. S. male civilian employees who desire to leave,

Please do not ask questions or request exceptions. There is no time for that. Read this Notice carefully. The word will NOT be passed over WGBY.

DO NOT USE YOUR TELEPHONE

Carry out the special evacuation instructions which have already been furnished to you and which you should have posted in your home. Specifically, pick up your pre-packed suitcases (not more than one per person). Include any special medicines, special foods and several changes of clothes. One blanket per person may be carried. Take I.D. cards, important legal and personal papers, check books, bank books, etc. Flashlights and transistor radios may be included. Tag all suitcases with your name and address. Have your two-part evacuation card filled out and ready to hand to the evacuation team when called for. Extra cards and shipping tags will be available at embarkation points. Busses will run continuously direct to the piers starting shortly after you receive this information until everyone is picked up. DO NOT PROCEED BY CAR. Leave your car at home with a tagged set of keys in the ignition or tied to the steering wheel. Tie up pets in the yard. YOU MAY NOT TAKE PETS WITH YOU. Leave house keys on table in the living room.

The evacuation will be by ship. There will be plenty of food and water and the best possible arrangements will be made for your comfort and quick return to the United States. You will be entirely safe. Your husbands are required for their military duties and may not be able to see you before departure. Friends and neighbors without small children are requested to help those with small children in every way both during the evacuation and aboard ship.

You will be given all possible assistance at the port of debarkation. Please keep calm and carry out all directions given you. The busses are starting their runs now. Get your suitcases and children and wait quietly in your front yard when ready.

God bless you. We will all miss you.

PUT THIS IN YOUR PURSE. DO NOT LEAVE IT LYING AROUND THE HOUSE OR YARD.

9-2   This message was hand-carried to dependents the morning of the evacuation … complete text is included in Chapter 9

59

10

Last in Line

It was a typical cloudless sky and 87 degrees of heat bathed Pier Victor as my two children and I stepped from the bus. The Pier was crawling with servicemen. I wondered where they all could have come from. Then I recalled my rude awakening amid the roar of C-130's early Sunday morning.

On Saturday, October 20, 1962, these transport jets had taken off from Cherry Point and Camp Lejeune, North Carolina heading for my back yard. Additionally, 2,400 rail cars were moving the heavy weapons of the tank division to the East Coast. It was the largest, swiftest, and most competent single military movement in the nation's history, involving more than 400,000 men, 200 warships, thousands of planes from all services, and a massive tonnage of guns and ammunition.

The United States was preparing to retaliate in minutes should Russia launch atomic war over Cuba—with more explosive tonnage than had been used in all the wars in history. However, President Kennedy had decreed no atomic bombs were to be used in an invasion of Cuba, should one be necessary. The Strategic Air Command's (SAC) nuclear deterrent stood at the ready should WWIII erupt, but Cuba was to be invaded with only the pre-Hiroshima explosives.

At 8:50 on Monday morning, October 22, 1962, officers of the Naval Air Station at McCalla Field, Guantanamo Bay, were summoned for a meeting with the Executive Officer. At approximately 9 a.m., Commander A. J. Rucker informed them of plans for evacuation of dependents. Each officer was provided with mimeographed sheets of instructions (a brief, secret notice to be handed to the wives which informed them this was not a drill), a small booklet to record addresses of any "not at home", and a black grease pencil to indicate evacuated quarters by marking them with a large 'V'.

Notification of dependents was scheduled to begin at 10 a.m., but there was a 'leak' at 9:20, so to thwart rumors and misinformaton from nonofficial sources, Captain Weber, Commanding Officer of the Naval Air Station, and CDR Rucker ordered the notification to begin immediately. This was when Colonel Killen, Commander of the Marine Barracks, called his wife, Chick.

It was an electrifying command to those of us who received this official notice to assemble for an evacuation in one hour. For the foreseeable future, our family life would be at an end. We were about to be abruptly thrust into the age-old role of war refugees.

At one of the quarters, an officer encountered a most incongruous sight. The long-awaited household effects of a family were being carried into their quarters from a truck. The unloading from the truck continued while the Navy wife calmly packed suitcases for herself and her children and prepared to evacuate.

Many children were still at school. Mothers were assured their children would be released from school and reach home prior to departure time of buses. Dependents first notified were ready for departure in less than the thirty minutes it took for the first buses to arrive for transport to the staging area. At no time were the buses forced to wait until someone had completed departure preparations.

After the buses departed, the evacuation team rechecked each house and put a large 'V' on each door with their black grease pencil, indicating the quarters had been vacated. In less than three hours, more than 2800 souls, every dependent woman and child, had been evacuated to the staging area. The youngest was four days old, and the oldest 62 years.

As my children and I stepped from the bus that hot October day, we joined a line on the dock at the staging area. The heat of the afternoon sun was intensified by the reflection from the cement walkway. I was grateful for the straw hat Chick had planted on Billy's head.

I heard a voice above the hubbub and shaded my eyes until the glare of light merged into the white-clad figure of a young sailor. He had hoisted himself onto a loading platform and was visible above the crowd, trying to make himself heard.
"Ladies, could I please have your attention for a moment?"
How could he be so presumptuous, I thought, as to expect us to focus our attention on him, when our emotions were making it difficult for us to focus at all.
"Ladies . . .", the sailor began again, "if you will lay claim to which baggage is yours, we'll carry it into this shed so you can have some shade."
Two sailors immediately approached me in line, and I pointed out the three suitcases and roll of blankets that were ours. They carried these into the shade of the storage shed as we followed.

After we were relocated, I asked one of the sailors if I should get back in line. "You can if you want to Lady," he replied gently, "but I don't think you'll get left behind, even if you're **last** in line." His answer brought the reality of our situation sharply into focus. This was **not** a drill.

In the center of the shed, sailors began ladling large malt-sized paper cups of ice water from shiny new galvanized garbage cans. This was welcome refreshment, indeed! I wondered who could have thought to provide it. Then I remembered briefly nodding to Rear Admiral Edward J. O'Donnell, Commander of the Naval Base, as I lined up with the others. His attention was on the women and children standing in the sun.

It was shortly after the Admiral's appearance that the sailor had told us to lay claim to our luggage and move into the storage shed. And, in the comparative comfort of the shade, listening to the eager gulping of my children, I could not help but marvel at the supreme thoughtfulness of the man who was executing orders from the Commander in Chief, and yet had taken the time to come personally to the pier and dispense ice water.

After a couple of hours, a large enough gap had been created in the crowd for me to see the gangplank through the doorway of the storage shed. As I leaned down to push our luggage forward, I glanced behind me to see how many others were still in the shed. There were only about thirty people at the most. I knew we had been the last busload to leave our area. It was diverting to think of myself as one of the last thirty dependents to leave the Base.

The last "evacuees" (there is that hateful word) have finally squeezed aboard the *Upshur,* and you "men of decision" are free to do as you see fit to defend our principles. You are free to blow the Island of Cuba off the face of the earth, and with it, the man I love!

11

The Commander in Chief

Brigadier General William T. Fairbourn, commander of the 5th Marine Expeditionary Brigade, was briefing his officers. He gave them orders to transport thousands of Marines to the Caribbean through the Panama Canal in a 19-ship convoy with destroyer escort. After he had been speaking for a few minutes, he switched on a television set, saying, "And now, it is my pleasure to introduce the next briefing officer."

The next briefing officer was the Commander in Chief, President John F. Kennedy, speaking from the White House. The American people had been told the President would be speaking to them that night on a matter of highest national urgency. The timing of his television address had required a sophisticated, and carefully orchestrated count down that began on October 21, 1962, shortly after the first C-130 transport had made its dramatic appearance over my backyard.

Early on that Sunday morning, while a golden autumn haze lay on the District of Columbia, strange activities were taking place. At 7:15 a.m., a motorist was driving past the old hotel in DC that houses the Fifth Army headquarters. He noticed soldiers in freshly pressed uniforms hurrying inside. At that moment, a voice from his car radio announced:
The Fifth Army denies it has been ordered on alert.

In Key West Florida, workers hastily constructed a control tower on the small airfield. A local lumberyard opened Sunday to supply materials. Unseen by the public, troops were on the move in destroyers, cruisers, and carriers, headed for stations along the Atlantic and Caribbean approaches to Cuba.

As the President bowed his head at mass Sunday morning, Secretary of Defense, Robert McNamara, was studying new photos of lethal missiles in Cuba. Films were taken to an 11 a.m. meeting at the White House. There, the President made his final decision in spite of stridently differing opinions to the contrary. He would order a *'quarantine'* of Cuba. 'Quarantine' was a softer term than 'blockade', which could be interpreted as an act of war.

Early that same morning, calls in the name of the President were made to 18 legislative leaders, requesting their presence in DC. Some were plucked from fishing trips by helicopter. An airlift for congressional chiefs had been plotted Sunday, positioning planes across the country. Senator Thomas Kuchel of California (the Republican whip) was found campaigning in San Diego. House Speaker John W. McCormack climbed aboard a plane at Boston. Senator Hubert Humphrey (Democratic whip) was picked up in Minneapolis by a four-seater jet trainer, which then plucked Rep Charles Halleck, (House leader) from the airport at Sioux Falls South Dakota, where he had been pheasant hunting. This same jet hopped over to Cedar Rapids, Iowa, where Senator Bourke Hickenlooper (Democrat from Iowa) was waiting.

House Democratic Whip, Hale Boggs of Louisiana, was fishing with a federal judge in the Gulf of Mexico when an air Force plane buzzed him and dropped a plastic bottle near his charter boat. A message inside the red-tagged bottle read: *Call Lawrence O'Brien. Urgent Message from the President of the U.S.* Then a helicopter landed on a nearby oilrig. A man with a megaphone began shouting at Boggs. The fishing boat maneuvered close to the oil drill and Boggs climbed a 100-foot steep ladder to the platform. The helicopter flew him to New Orleans, where he took a twin-seat jet fighter and streaked to Washington.

At noon, President Kennedy broke off his conferences and paper signing to swim in the White House pool. He swam slowly up and down, doing the first two laps with a crawl, then switching to a more leisurely breast stroke.

In New York, Adlai Stevenson's office at the United Nations began to resemble a Military command post. Arthur Schlesinger came up from the White House to help prepare Stevenson's big speech to the UN Security Council. A State Department aide, two CIA officers, and two photo-interpretation experts augmented the small group on Stevenson's staff who were in on the secret.

The most overwhelming concern was that the Russians might get wind of the operation and make a peremptory move, so Gromyko was followed to Idelwilde Airport where he was flying back to Russia at 2 p.m. A special assistant to the White House reported Gromyko took off on schedule, after making an innocuous planeside statement, apparently unaware of the impending American action.

By Sunday evening, the dinner party circuit was electric with rumor and excitement. Pentagon officials began to sleep in their offices on cots. A reporter who discovered a cot being moved into the office of Nils Lennartson, a Defense deputy assistant secretary, was told that Lennartson had a sore foot and had to rest. McNamara retired to his cot at 10 p.m. but was awakened shortly thereafter with new problems about the blockade that kept him up another hour.

Secrecy still shuttered armed preparations on Monday, October 22. Men were roused from their beds in the wee hours. It was a day of swiftly rising tempo and unbearable tension. Continuous meetings of Pentagon Joint Chiefs were in session as blockade developments unfolded. In a Navy flag plot, an Admiral watched the chart as the ships of his newly designed Task Force steamed into position

U.S. military units around the world were alerted. President Kennedy phoned former Presidents Eisenhower, Truman, and Hoover, and personally told them, "Here's what I have decided to do."

World leaders were notified by our ambassadors. The earliest to be briefed, as a matter of courtesy, were Prime Minister Harold MacMillan, French President Charles deGaulle, and German Chancellor Konrad Adenaur. The Latin American Ambassador was summoned to the White House.

Another White House meeting that afternoon coordinated endless details. The hour of the President's speech was dubbed "P-Hour" and all plans were aimed at that moment.

The White House had confidentially asked top network officials for radio and TV time Monday night. Don Wilson, Deputy Director of the U.S. Information Agency, asked telephone company officials to make secret connections with 11 radio stations in 9 cities so the stations could beam Spanish translations of the President's speech to Cuba and South America.

Newsmen were closing in on the White House. Secrecy was vital. McNamara personally called John Hay Whitney, owner of the New York Herald Tribune, to solicit his cooperation.

Shortly after 4 p.m., the Russian Ambassador was summoned to the State Department, where he was handed the President's speech and a letter for Khrushchev. At 4:15 p.m., 46 allied ambassadors were briefed in a State Department conference room.

At the White House, meetings of National Security Council, Cabinet, and Legislative leaders were held in rapid succession just before the President's 7 p.m speech. This meeting was short. Some argued for an all-out invasion of Cuba immediately. The President calmly defended his decision.

As minutes ticked toward 7 p.m., Pierre Salinger and Newton Minow, chairman of the FCC called managers of the 11 stations selected to broadcast the speech in Spanish. When they protested they had no cut-in facilities, Salinger revealed the lines had already been laid. Later, Americans tuning to these stations were startled to hear a voice speaking in Spanish.

At the State Department, a complicated "scenario" was being followed to the minute. Messages had gone out on Sunday, October 21, to all our missions abroad, and now the ambassadors were told to inform foreign offices of America's decision. Dean Acheson had flown to Paris and personally informed President Charles de Gaulle.

The President, in his study, was ready for the speech. A door was closed to shut out a murmur of voices. His secretary, Ms. Evelyn Lincoln, handed him a brush. He swept it through his mop of hair. An imperious technical finger leveled at him.

During his remarkable 17-minute speech, President Kennedy outlined his decision for a quarantine of ships enroute to Cuba, demanding that Khrushchev dismantle the soviet military bases there and remove the lethal nuclear missiles and bombers from the island. He ended it as follows:

"The cost of freedom is always high--- but Americans have always paid it. ... Our goal is not the victory of might but the vindication of right --- not peace at the expense of freedom, but both peace and freedom, here in this Hemisphere and, we hope, around the world. God willing, that goal will be achieved."

As he concluded his address, our ship had barely pulled away from the dock at Guantanamo Bay.

12

First Night Aboard Ship

Through a maze of crowded corridors, I endeavored to follow the two sailors who were carrying our gear. Because of the crowd, it was necessary for my children and me to go single file, and while keeping my eyes on them, I lost track of one of our luggage carriers. I followed the other sailor through the lounge and into a large troop compartment stacked four deep with bunks. He told me to find a bunk for myself and my children, and promised the other sailor with the third suitcase and bedroll would find me.

I settled Colleen and Billy on the suitcases with their dolls and searched up and down all the narrow aisles looking for a bunk that did not have either a person or a possession on it, finally finding a top bunk with very little space between it and the overhead pipes. I made one exploratory step up onto the lowest bunk, thinking to put something on the top one to save it. Then I realized how ridiculous this location was. I could never lift my children up onto it, and if I did, I would have to stand guard beside it constantly to see that they didn't roll off. I went back to the children, and after waiting for what seemed an interminable period, took them by the hand and went in search of the other sailor.

Outside this troop compartment was the lounge with every square inch occupied by confused women and children. In one corner, I spotted my neighbors (Chick Killen, Claire Seibert, Barbara McCarthy, Mickie Hagen, and Betty Gentry). I decided right then and there that more than clothing or a place to sleep, I needed familiar companionship for moral support. We joined them. The second sailor with our bedroll and last piece of luggage found me. I left the children with my colleagues while I retrieved our other two suitcases from the troop compartment.

As I rejoined my neighbors, a voice came over the loudspeaker asking for attention. There was silence and we heard the voice of Admiral O'Donnell. He read us the following message from the Chief of Naval Operations, Admiral George Anderson:

The calm and serene manner in which you have accepted the threat of possible personal danger while living at Guantanamo has been viewed with admiration and respect. Now our judgment dictates that you should leave the scene of increasing danger to your own safety. I am sure you will accept this action with the same fine spirit that has been so obvious throughout your stay at Guantanamo. Rest assured that we will do all possible to provide for your welfare in the days ahead.

Shortly thereafter, we heard the ominous grinding and groaning as the big ship began to move away from the dock. It was nearly 5 p.m. and a flawlessly blue late afternoon sky was on view through the portholes. Claire, holding Mickie Hagen's baby, turned abruptly from a porthole, blinking rapidly.

"Funniest thing," she said, not looking amused at all, "everytime I look out the porthole I get tears in my eyes."

So, the last of the 2,811 dependents were underway at just before 5 p.m. on October 22, 1962. Among the 1,703 aboard the *Upshur* were 200 babies under two years, 735 young boys and girls, 168 teen-agers, 25 men and 580 wives. Earlier, 339 dependents had left in five military Air Transports and arrived in Norfolk, Virginia before midnight that same night. Three other ships . . . the seaplane tender *Duxbury Bay*, the refrigeration ship, *Hyadies*, and the tank landing ship,

DeSoto County . . . carried a total of 629 dependents. They left earlier Monday, but the larger and faster *Upshur* was to eventually overtake them. We were ordered to travel in convoy with a destroyer escort until we got out of dangerous waters, which meant the *Upshur* was not travelling at capacity speed until noon on Tuesday, October 23, when we finally reached friendly waters. I did not, of course, know any of this until later.

As we waited in the ship's troop lounge for some word about where we could move ourselves and our belongings for the three-day trip, through the crowd I noticed a young mother across the room kneeling on the floor. She laid down a raincoat, and with one hand, tried to smooth it out. From her shoulder, she tenderly placed her sleeping baby on the raincoat. Turning into the crowd and, still kneeling, she took a crying infant from the arms of a very pale young woman. The latter, relieved of her crying infant, stumbled through the crowd to a doorway, where she collapsed on a step, her head in her lap. The first mother continued to kneel on the floor, comforting the crying infant and hovering protectively over her own baby asleep on the floor. It was these woman who suffered most during the evacuation . . . the ones with babes in arms, requiring diapers and bottles.

As we waited, Chick Killen brought a bed sheet from the bunk she had finally been assigned and spread it out on the floor for our little ones. Among the five wives of Marine Officers, there were five toddlers, one baby, two boys under 12, and three teen-ages. Beth and Kay Seibert performed full-time complementary baby-sitting for any mother who needed them. George Killen, Jr. helped in the mess hall. If medals were given to civilians for the evacuation, they belong to all the teen-agers aboard the *Upshur* who volunteered for mess duty, lavatory clean-up, and baby-sitting. God bless them all!

Eventually, bunks were found for the remaining five Marine officer's families aboard the *Upshur*. We were ensconced in troop compartment B-7, located clear to the back and bottom of the ship. It was a large circular room, containing about 150 bunks, four deep. In the center of the room were two water faucets with small basins, and in one corner, a deep utility sink. I bathed my children in the latter, as the troop shower was up two flights, and my children were accustomed to tub baths, not showers.

I secured two bottom bunks across the aisle from each other for my children, and I took one on the third tier. This was a sheer luxury. We each had a bunk to call our own with clean bedding. I unrolled the children's special blankets from our bedroll, and they were so ecstatic to see them it almost made dragging that bedroll seem worth it. Curled up with their familiar 'blankies' and a thumb, they were asleep almost immediately. The unfamiliarity of the day had exhausted them.

That first night aboard, after the children were asleep, we five Marine wives congregated in one corner of compartment B-7. Claire rubbed her forehead and I asked if she'd like something for her headache. She spoke for all evacuees when she said, "My head aches, my arms ache, my back and legs ache . . . but most of all, my heart aches, and there's nothing I can take for that!"

13

The Fire Drill

During the three days aboard ship, we ate in the troop mess in three shifts, waiting in long lines in a narrow hallway. We were allowed to enter only when enough people had left the Mess Hall to create space for the next seating. The meals, served cafeteria style, were ample and tasty.

Sailors in the mess hall were most helpful in carrying our trays, escorting us to tables, and even tying on the children's bibs. It was an unpalatable task for combat-ready troops, but they all carried it out with a smile. Teen-age passengers also assisted in the serving and clean-up, which facilitated rapid turnover between seatings.

One of the valuable decisions I made in my frantic packing frenzy was to throw in the children's small silverware, thinking it might be a welcome sight to them. I also remembered the smallest spoon on a troop transport was a tablespoon, which would not even fit into either of their mouths. In my overwrought state, at least twice, those serving in the cafeteria had to chase after me because I had left the children's utensils on the trays.

Since it was an MSTS (Military Sea Transport Ship), the *Upshur* contained several cabins with attached bathrooms. These went on a first-come, first-served basis, until after the ship was underway. At that time, the Chaplains aboard asked those in cabins if they would be willing to relinquish these luxurious spaces to the women with infants and small children. With only one exception (and believe me, we all knew the name of the woman who refused) every occupant willingly gave up her more comfortable space in deference to those in greater need. This was only one of many altruistic gestures among those living through an arduous situation in close proximity.

At noon on Tuesday, October 23, 1962, an announcement came across the ship's sound system that a telegram had been received from President Kennedy. We all stopped in our tracks, and stood quietly as his message was read. It follows:

To you who have had to leave your homes at Guantanamo for an indefinite period, I send my deep regrets. I know you do so with sadness, for some of you also leave behind your husband; others your father --- and you who have been civilian employees are uprooted from your job as well as your homes. It is my most earnest hope that circumstances will permit your return. I send my warmest greetings and best wishes to you and those you leave behind.

As it was read, I fought to keep back the tears. It was emotionally the most difficult moment of the entire trip for me, as I'd allowed myself no time for reflection before then. In retrospect, I am awed that during his impossibly busy 154 hours, the President of the United States had time to remember us. Yet again, I am certain it was no coincidence that during those 154 hours when he insisted upon absolute secrecy, we were not far from his thoughts. He had delayed his P-Hour speech until every dependent was safely off the island of Cuba and under the protective wing of a destroyer escort.

About 2 p.m. that first full day of sailing, another announcement came across the loudspeaker requesting that all children under 14 (mothers as necessary) assemble in the main lounge in 15 minutes. At the appointed time, one of the ship's crew told a story about the proud history of the *Upshur* and her role

75

in the Navy. Then, with great solemnity, he requested the children raise their right hands and recite an allegiance for induction into the *Upshur Club.*

At the conclusion of this ceremony, assisted by teenage passengers, each child was handed cookies, punch, and an *Upshur Club* badge. This tin badge was about four inches in circumference, white with blue lettering. In the Mess Hall thereafter, *Upshur Club* badges were displayed in abundance. Those who wore them seemed to walk taller for being made to feel part of the "team".

My children and I had to climb two ships ladders from the hold of the ship to reach the nearest toilets. In spite of this, Billy, who had been out of diapers only a month, never had an accident. We women and children in the hold of the ship were assigned the men's 'head,' usually reserved for troops being transported. On one occasion, I came out of a stall and observed my two-year-old son industriously washing his hands . . . in the urinal.

Although it was only two ships ladders to the toilet, we had to climb those two ships ladders plus two flights of stairs before reaching the lowest access to fresh air so critical to Colleen, my three-year old. She had become seasick the first morning. Since I was not similarly afflicted, others told me the remedy . . . fresh air as soon after she arises as possible.

Thereafter, the woman in the bunk across from me would come over first thing every morning and offer me a soda cracker from among her precious ration. She informed me that eating this would allow Colleen to climb from the hold of the ship to the first deck before her little stomach turned inside out. I don't think this woman and I even exchanged names, but it was a corporal act of mercy I shall never forget, as there were no crackers available on the ship and I had brought none. The only thing Colleen was able to keep down the whole trip besides those crackers was some noodles, rice, and grits.

On the last morning aboard, I glanced out the porthole while we were eating breakfast. There were no portholes in compartment B-7. I noticed a barge alongside the *Upshur*, and as I stood up to take a closer look, I saw large cardboard boxes being hoisted aboard by high-line. One of the servicemen told me it was the *Opportune*, a fleet tug, transferring clothing donated by Tidewater Navy/Marine Wives' Clubs and civilians in Virginia.

It is difficult for me to explain how deeply this thoughtful gesture affected me. Most of us had not come prepared for winter weather, and knowing this, the Military in Norfolk had sent out a plea for clean, mended, warm clothing for the evacuees. I had not packed any winter clothing for my children, because there was none that still fit them, so the 40-degree temperatures predicted in Norfolk were a real concern to me. I'll never forget the red plaid fleece-lined jacket with matching hood that I found to fit my daughter, and a similar warm garment in her brother's size. I later learned the donations had been so plentiful, a message had to be issued that no more would be needed.

The *Upshur* was air-conditioned, and even with the extremely crowded conditions, fairly comfortable. Life was not so rosy aboard the other ships. Karen, the wife of Captain Calvin M. Morris of the Marine Barracks, shared with me the experiences she and her children encountered aboard the *Duxbury Bay*.

Because Karen's home was just off Sherman Avenue (the main road of the Naval Base) she and her children were on one of the earliest buses that left our area, known as Marine Point. We other Marine wives were further down the block, in the cul de sac, so were picked up last. Karen's ship sailed about 4 p.m., and as if the passengers weren't traumatized enough, shortly after departure, over the loudspeaker came the order, "Man the anti-aircraft. Assume battle positions!"

The *Duxbury Bay* was not air-conditioned. Karen found one bunk, third level up, for herself and three children, ages 11 months, 3, and 4 years. She spent the first night aboard standing in the aisle beside this bunk, pushing bottoms back onto it, as the ship was bucking badly. When one child would finally get to sleep, the others would awaken the sleeping child, and of course, Karen stood the whole night in an aisle about one and a half feet wide.

The only toilet and drinking fountain were clear at the other end of the Duxbury Bay, accessed through aisles thick with traffic. There were 350 dependents aboard. Karen and all three of her children were sick at the same time the first morning. Another woman observing her plight, came to her rescue. She and one of the ship's crew found an office where Karen and her children could sleep on the floor. Although the ship's doctor gave them pills, none of them lost their sea-sickness the whole trip. Karen was unaware that she was pregnant with her fourth child.

For me, personally, the only hardship aboard the Upshur were the never-ending stairs my children had to climb . . . for meals . . . for the toilet . . . for the air my daughter needed . . . and for the firedrill. When the fire alarm sounded, the 300 women and children in compartment B-7 scrambled for the single ships ladder.

I took the two life jackets issued to me, and knelt down to thread the straps around Colleen's tiny body first. I had been told I could carry Billy, so he would not need a jacket. By the time I had put on my life jacket, the one I had laced onto Colleen was down around her knees, as there was nothing but adult-sized life jackets aboard. It was then I made up my mind to simply sit this one out.

I sat down on the nearest bunk and began telling my children a story. We were thus involved when a sailor came down the ships ladder and spotted me.
"Ma'am", he said. "Why aren't you up on deck?"
I can remember my reply as clearly as if it was yesterday. I said, "If this ship goes down, I'm going down with it!"
"Ma'am", he entreated. "You have to join the others on deck." I didn't move.

Another sailor swung down the ship's ladder, hanging onto the railing with one hand. "What's up?" he said, nodding his head in our direction. The first sailor explained the situation. I hadn't moved.
"Ma'am", the second sailor pleaded, "the 'All-Clear' can't be sounded until all those from *every* station are on deck."
Sensing the discomfort this could cause my fellow passengers, I tied the life jacket around my daughter's small body as best I could, ignoring the threading devices that were spaced too far apart. Then, I guided Colleen toward the ladder. She advanced forward, tripped over the dangling ties, and fell.

At this point, Colleen turned around and crawled back to me. I guessed it must have been against regulations for one of the sailors to help me, so I said to my daughter,

"Colleen, this is a game. If you can climb to the top of the stairs, Mommy will give you a prize."

She could not pretend to walk swaddled in the cumbersome life jacket, but with the greatest resolve, she began crawling on her hands and knees toward the ship's ladder. Once there, still on hands and knees, she began her ascent, stopping to remove the long ties of the life jacket out from beneath her knees and hands as she advanced. Carrying her brother, I walked carefully behind her to ensure that if she lost her balance, my legs would break her fall.

The two ship's ladders seemed steeper than I had remembered them, and then we had to ascend the two flights of stairs before finally arriving on deck. On reaching our destination, Colleen turned to me with a look of triumph, and I praised her lavishly. Luckily I had a package of lifesavers (ironically enough), and gave her one as her prize, telling her again how well she had done. She was obviously delighted with her achievement.

Remembering this incident later in her life, I remarked to Colleen it was the first time I had really thought about her as an entity apart from me, with a will and a mind of her own. In that moment, I regarded her with a new respect, an epiphany that changed my way of relating to my children from that point forward. As Kahlil Gibran so aptly put it in <u>The Prophet:</u>

"Your children . . . come through you but not from you
and though they are with you
yet they belong not to you.
You may give them your love
but not your thoughts
For they have their own thoughts."

13-1   Colleen and Billy sitting on deck chair aboard the
        Upshur

13-2

Copy of the
high-line transfer
of clothing from
a fleet tug to the
Upshur a few
hours before it
docked at
Norfolk

14

The Turning Point

As the prow of the Upshur was slicing through calm waters on the moonlit night of October 24th, we onboard were not aware that this date would go down in history as the most tense moment of the entire Crisis period.

It was the impending 'quarantine' and whether it would be honored by the Cubans and Russians that most seriously concerned our national leaders. Could those poised for battle on both sides of the fence hold their fire? Would the Russian ships on their way to Cuba obey the quarantine? There were 16 U.S. Naval destroyers and 3 cruise ships forming a 500-mile arc interrupting access to the East Coast of Cuba. The 25 Soviet merchant ships headed there were staying on course.

The key ship in this approaching armada was the new Russian motor vessel, the *Poltava,* an 18,000-ton cargo carrier with a roomy hold and modern unloading equipment. Based on her profile, the Pentagon suspected the *Poltava* was carrying intermediate range rockets and nuclear warheads to Cuba.

Manned by a crew of 41, the *Poltava* was moving southwest in the Atlantic at her 17-knot cruising speed when the cruiser Newport News and destroyers Keith and Lawrence were ordered to intercept the Russian cargo ship. On the night of October 22, the blockade Commander, Vice Admiral Alfred G. (Corky) Ward, aboard the *Newport News,* ordered a speed of 27 knots. It taxed the boilers of the other two ships in the armada to keep up.

In his flag cabin, as head of Task Force 136, Ward had pictures of the *Poltava* and a sheaf of intelligence data about her probable cargo. Defense Secretary Robert S. McNamara had issued "fire if necessary" orders to halt Russian ships. If Russia meant to go to war to get her ships through, the Vice Admiral knew the *Poltava* could be the spark. Realizing his decision concerning whether to fire or let the *Poltava* proceed could be the potential for a global holocaust, it was Ward's personal intention to proceed with extreme caution. He intended to intercept the *Poltava* himself and direct the boarding party.

Early on the morning of Oct. 24th, radars on the flagship picked up a ship moving on a direct line for Cuba. A check with the sea surveillance computer in Norfolk confirmed it was the target, the *Poltava*.
"Stay loose and be ready", Ward signaled his flanking destroyers. The Russian and U.S. Navy ships were closing fast. At their present rates of speed, confrontation of the two great powers on the high seas would soon be inevitable.

Shortly before noon, with the *Poltava* little more than two hours sailing time away, tension mounted. And then, although barely discernible because of its size, the 18,000-ton cargo carrier began a slow arc in the aqua blue waters. It took awhile for the massive vessel to complete its turn, but when it had, it was heading northeast, the direction from which it had come.

As it became clear that the *Poltava* and her crew of 41 were heading back the way they had come, the Vice Admiral got the other destroyer skippers on voice radio, and in his soft drawl announced,
"Our friend has turned back".

From then on, Khrushchev's course ran downhill. Other ships turned back. Some stayed dead in the water for several days, awaiting orders. Some, after allowing searches by U.S. boarding parties, were determined to be carrying non-military cargoes, and were allowed to proceed to Cuba. Four days later, Khrushchev agreed to dismantle his Cuban missile sites.

Although it was the war we never fought, the Cuban operation had its hours of bravery and sadness. Air Force, Navy, and Marine pilots skimmed treetops under Cuban anti-aircraft fire to take pictures of the missile sites. On one such picture-taking mission, Air Force Major Rudolf Anderson, Jr. was killed. Operational crashes also took some lives.

But the dam of tension broke on October 25th when Admiral George W. Anderson, Jr., chief of Naval Operations received telephoned word from Admiral Robert L. Dennison in Norfolk, relayed by Vice Admiral Ward, that some of the communist bloc ships on the Cuba run were turning back. By the time the *Upshur* landed in Norfolk, the world was breathing a bit more easily. The war we never fought was over before it began.

---

[1] Knebel, Fletcher, "The War We Never Fought – Tribune Exclusive – February 7 –10, 1963 (co-author of "Seven Days in May").

WEDNESDAY   -:-   USNS UPSHUR   -:-   24 OCT 62

RADIO PRESS TO COMMANDERS VESSELS SUBSCRIBING TO THE UNITED PRESS
INTERNATIONAL RCA NEWS SERVICE OCTOBER 23, 1962.

SHOWDOWN NEAR ON CUBA, RED SHIPS SAIL TOWARD NAVY"
WASHINGTON--- THE UNITED STATES AND RUSSIA HAVE HEADED INTO A POSSIBLE
MILITARY SHOWDOWN AS SOME 20 COMMUNIST SHIPS BORE DOWN ON A U.S.
ATLANTIC FLEET PLEDGED TO HALT AND SEARCH THEM. THE FACE TO FACE
TENSE OF WILL IN PERHAPS THE GRAVEST CRISIS OF THE ATOMIC AGE COULD
COME SOMEWHERE IN CARIBBEAN WATERS. IF THE SOVIET VESSELS REFUSE TO
BE SEARCHED FOR OFFENSIVE ARMS BEING CARRIED TO CUBA, U.S. WARSHIPS
ARE UNDER ORDERS TO SINK THEM. AT LEAST 40 U.S. SHIPS AND 20,000
MEN WERE IN THE CARIBBEAN AREA. A SPECIAL TARGET OF THE U.S. BLOCKAD-
ERS WAS A HUGE SOVIET SHIP PRESUMABLY RIGGED TO CARRY THE 1,000
OR 2,000 MILE MISSILES THAT PRESIDENT KENNEDY SAID POSED A THREAT
TO ALL THE WESTERN HEMISPHERE.

MOSCOW--- THE SOVIET UNION, IN SWIFT REACTION TO THE U.S. BLOCKADE OF
CUBA, HAS CANCELLED ALL TROOP LEAVES, ORDERED THE ENTIRE COMMUNIST
BLOC TO STEP UP ITS MILITARY PREPAREDNESS AND ACCUSED THE UNITED STAT-
ES OF "TAKING A STEP ALONG THE ROAD OF UNLEASHING A THERMONUCLEAR
WORLD WAR." THE SOVIET CALLED A MEETING OF MILITARY LEADERS OF THE
EIGHT NATION WARSAW PACT, THE "COMMUNIST NATO,"   AND ORDERED
THE "UNITED ARMED FORCES" OF THE SOVIET BLOC TO INCREASE THEIR LAND
AND NAVAL PREPARDNESS.

14-1 Press coverage from aboard ship as Quarantine activities heated up

15

Arrival in Norfolk

During the long days aboard ship, the children would often ask, "Mama, where are we going?" The mantra I would repeat, with assurance and enthusiasm was, "We're going to our new house." How else was I to explain something I didn't even know myself! I would repeat this evasion as often as necessary, elaborating as I went along. Their questioning was so insistent and I repeated it so often, I almost came to believe it myself.

Our arrival in Norfolk the evening of October 25th was heralded with an air of celebration that seemed incongruous to the circumstances. Crowds stood on the pier waving. Uniformed bands played. We all came up from the bowels of the ship and crowded on deck, angling for a place near the edge to watch the *Upshur* nose into the slip.

It was a misty 42 degrees, with a slight drizzle as I stood on the deck with definite feelings of ambivalence about the celebration. Shortly thereafter, the children and I were herded into tight stuffy corridors where we stood crammed together for over an hour waiting to disembark. We could move neither forward nor backward, and had no idea what was going on, as there were no portholes in the corridors leading to the gangplank.

We later learned the delay was occasioned by media interviews of those first off the ship. In fact, flashbulbs greeted me as I walked down the gangplank wearing my wool suit and the straw hat Chick had loaned Billy. Chick was, after all, the Colonel's wife and I was not going to abandon her hat in the hold of the ship.

This photographic evidence of my arrival was sent out over UP wire photo and published in several papers, but after three days and nights aboard that crowded ship, I did not want my picture in the newspaper. All I wanted was to get off that ship as rapidly as possible, settle my children, see a newspaper, and try to find out what had happened to my husband!

Officials must have realized delays for media coverage were the last straw for travel-weary passengers, because when Karen Morris arrived at 11 p.m. on the *Duxbury Bay*, disembarkation was immediate, with passengers escorted off between a human chain of Marines who admitted no newspaper reporters or cameras. Baggage was taken off later and transported for them separately.

*

Guantanamo Bay, Cuba

Dearest Patsy,

I hope the trip was not too hard for you and the kids. I'm sorry that I wasn't more help and didn't stay around longer. The reason I left is because I was afraid one of us might break down in front of the children.

Things are not yet back to normal here and I don't expect that for some time. The Cuban workers came back onto the Base today so things must be quiet on the other side. We continue to prepare for defense of the Base but none of us really believes that Castro will commit his troops against us. He talks, but I don't feel he has the same hold on the people as he had in the past.

It looks as if this will be a long and drawn out process. Since I will be here for some time, I think you should look into renting a place for you and the kids until I can join you. Let me know as soon as you can so I can send the 500-pound express shipment direct. I do think I should include the washer if at all possible. What do you think?

I went back into the house yesterday and it seemed strange. It was as if you had just left and were visiting one of the neighbors. The kids must have been on the circle. I didn't stay. Right now I live in the office. Don't want to go back into the house unless I have to. I took out the clothes I wanted. Routed around and found some of the snapshots of you and the kids. Put them in the pack and left.

Before you ask, I don't know how long my tour will be under these new conditions. It could vary from 12 to 20 months. As you probably know, the President has frozen all tours for the next 12 months.

I don't want you to worry about me. I am fine and don't think there is the slightest possibility that I'll become involved in any fighting. I'm back in my old job and not directly involved with the Defense Forces per se. Somebody has to "mind the store" and I'm the guy.

Colonel Seibert has given me a completely free hand to operate as I please. All I have to do is to tell him what action I have taken. There was some pressure to get me into a job with the Ground Defense Force Headquarters but Colonel Killen put his foot down and said that I was not available in any capacity ... that my job was Marine Barracks Supply Officer, and that as long as he had command, he was not going to allow me to be moved.

I looked on the manifests of all the ships but did not see your name. Guess you forgot to drop off the bottom half of the boarding ticket. Bill Hubbard said he thought you got aboard the *Upshur*. Did you contact Edythe and CM in Norfolk? I meant to suggest it and give you their address, but when I came back to the house, you were gone.

I tried to send a cable but the shop has been closed the past couple of days. And of all times, the "ham" radio is out of order. Sure hope they get that fixed.

Tibbs, as well as the other horses, have been turned out to pasture for the present. Since the Cubans are back now to some extent, I'll try to get up there and see what the deal is.

Take care of yourself and the kids. Can't afford to have anything happen to you and them. And for goodness sakes, don't worry about me. I'm all right and I intend to stay that way.   Love, Bill

*

We finally walked down the gangplank at approximately 5:30 p.m., having docked about 4 o'clock. The stiff breeze accompanying the 42-degree temperature was a definite shock after three months of tropical weather. In the next two weeks, the skin over my entire body peeled as if I had a sunburn. Thankfully, we were immediately escorted onto heated Virginia Transit Company buses and transported to Barracks No 3602 at Little Creek Naval Amphibious Base, Virginia, which would serve as the staging area until transportation was available to take evacuees elsewhere. I remember very little about this 45-minute bus trip. With the relief of finally having 'arrived' (whatever that meant), I think the children and I immediately fell asleep.

When we arrived at the barracks, we encountered several lines. I was instructed to join the line behind the first initial of our last name. This operation was well organized, with large signs posted overhead indicating the letters of the alphabet represented by each line. I joined the appropriate line, and after only a five-minute wait, gave my name to the woman behind the table.

We didn't know it, but the manifest of the ship had been distributed broadly to all service personnel in the vicinity, and after I had given my name, the woman grabbed a roster, and said, "Oh, yes, Mrs. Kendig. Three people want you." As she passed the list across to me, I couldn't even see their names my eyes were so blurred with tears. Folks in the area not only knew me, but were willing to give me sanctuary! I was so overcome I thought I was going to bawl!

I put my hand over my mouth to choke back the tears because there were others in line behind me. The names finally swam into focus. One offer came from my husband's cousins who I'd never met, but whose names I knew (Naval Commander C.M. Briggs and his wife, Edythe). Another was made by former neighbors from Camp LeJeune (Captain William Longshaw and his wife, Betsy), and the last offer was from dear Marine friends who had become the Godparents of our son, Billy. I had not known they were recently transferred to Norfolk. I told the lady Chief Warrant Officer Lester W. Kuchler and his wife, Trudy, were our choice. She made a quick telephone call, told me they were on their way, and explained where we should wait.

As we proceeded to the rendezvous point, a representative from the American Red Cross approached me and asked my name. After consulting a list, she handed me a card with a toll free number I could use to make three free telephone calls anywhere in the United States. She also indicated the Red Cross would send an "All is ok" cable to my husband in Guantanamo. I marveled at such an invaluable service rendered so inconspicuously! As a former employee of the National Red Cross on the Island of Okinawa from 1956 to 1958, I felt a new surge of pride at having been associated with an organization that so effectively delivers service where and when it is needed most.

I took my children to a sofa in the rendezvous point, handed them their familiar blankets, and told them I would be right back. I saw phone booths only steps away, and stood in a line for one of them. I first called my parents, who were extremely relieved to hear my voice. We didn't talk long, as there were others waiting to make calls. My husband's parents were glad to hear from me but expressed deep concern about their son. I repeated to them what he had said to me . . . that he would be the guy in the rear with the gear.

When I rejoined my children, I took one look at my daughter and knew it was a mistake to have left her even for a few minutes. Her lips were purple and drawn and she was shaking. My departure had been one incident too many for her. I pulled her gently into my arms and began rocking her and trying to reassure her. It was thus my friends found us. I looked up, and still cradling Colleen, fell into the open arms of Les Kuchler, who said, "Let's go home, Pat."

Upon arrival at their doorstep in Portsmouth, Virginia, we were warmly welcomed by the Kuchler's three children and their German shepherd. As we walked into their home, I still had Colleen tightly wrapped in my arms, trying to calm her. Les was carrying my son, Billy, who looked with wide eyes into their living room, a cozy and welcoming sight indeed. Candles were flickering on the mantle above a roaring fire. Their German Shepherd was wagging his tail in greeting.

Billy threw his arms up in the air, and said, "There's our new candles. There's our new dog".
Then much to the surprise of everyone but me, he pointed at their daughter, and said, "Get **out** of our new house!"

15-1   Author's arrival in Norfolk in straw hat … Colleen, far left; Billy in sailor's arms

15-2   Celebration at Norfolk on arrival of *Upshur*, October 25, 1962

16

Messages in a Bottle

October 27, 1962

Dearest Patsy,

I wrote you a rather long letter the other night but sent it to my folks address for the lack of a better one. I guess they will know where you are and forward it to you. I think staying close to the military is the best thing. Can't really see that we fit in the civilian life at all any more.

I sent a parcel post shipment of some things to you. It left here tonight by air. Don't really know what is in it, as Viola was in the other day to clean the house, and I asked her to pick out some things to send. I didn't have a chance to see what she chose. I'll have her start on the 500-pound shipment next.

I also want to prepare the car for shipment. Monday I will put the wheels in motion to get our furniture out of Camp Lejeune and on its way to you.

It's funny sitting here and watching all the fuss and hoopla about Cuba pass you by. We are just waiting. And all the while, the decisions about Cuba are being made elsewhere (Washington . . . the UN). Makes us sort of feel like 'spectators'.

Things are starting to slow down around here. Not quite as hectic as they were when you and the kids left. I think that the troops are starting to realize that we are not at the present time going out the gate into Cuba.

What is left of the Marine Barracks has really closed ranks.. We eat together most of the time, and now that things are getting back to normal, we even went to the movie together. Our clubhouse is the Colonel's office.

I find my days quite busy. Right now I'm trying to reeastablish the Marine Barracks as a separate unit not tied to the people who've come to *'visit'* with us. This has not been the easiest thing to do and I have had to lock horns with some senior officers to win my point. Thank goodness, Colonel Killen has backed me 100%. We are back to what we were originally assigned to do. When this flap started, I just opened the warehouse doors and everything went. You should see the place now. It's bare! Now we have to see how much stuff we actually issued and present a bill to the Ground Forces for repayment to the Marine Barracks. I really don't think we will ever account for it all, but we have to try.

Went up the other day to check on Tibbs. Gave him some wheat germ. I learned Special Service will buy all the horses from their owners. Will know Monday what they will offer for him.

The troops and I are living in the office now. Just as well, don't really like going back to the house with you and the kids not there. By the way, I hope that Colleen is eating again and that Billy is over that ear infection.

No word has come down concerning return of dependents to GTMO or to any change in the length of the tour. I really don't think that dependents will be allowed back here before the end of my tour. Curing the ills in Cuba is going to be a long and drawn out process.

I feel, as do the other people here, that the only way this mess can be cleaned up is for armed intervention. We know the risks involved. We know what can happen as a result. But still, we feel the only way to end this clear and present danger to our way of life is to overthrow this government now in power. This sounds like saber rattling and all of that, but I just can't see any other way. If the President can do it by negotiation, fine. I wish him well.

It is you . . . and the people like you . . . that make our country what it is. You could have a husband who is always home at night. You could have a home that is never disrupted by constant moves. You could have the peace of mind of knowing your husband will not be called out without notice and sent away. Maybe someday the other people in this country will come to appreciate the military team.

I put a lot of information in the letter I sent to my parent's home. Will write the folks and ask them to forward that letter to you c/o Edythe Briggs. Love, Bill

*

30 October 1962

Dearest Patsy,

Just a quick note. Wanted to get this $100 check in the mail to you as soon as possible. I'm sending it to the home of Edythe Briggs.

I haven't heard anything from you so far. Don't know where you are or how you made out on the trip. I know a letter must be in the mail, but none has arrived yet. More later.Love, Bill

*

31 October 1962

Dear Patsy –

You have me going around in circles. From your first letter, you told me that you were going to stay in the Norfolk area. Now you are talking about Utah. Frankly, I'm confused.

I have already sent the parcel post to you c/o the Briggs'. I am going to STOP all other shipments until I can find out just where the hell to send the stuff. Thank goodness I haven't completed the correspondence on getting the furniture out of permanent storage. I had also made arrangements to have the car shipped to Norfolk for your use.

If you want to go to Salt Lake, that is fine, but Pat, please make up your mind. I don't know where I can even locate you. I have letters sent to my folks, to the Briggs', now to Kuchler. The check for $100, incidentally, was sent to Briggs'. All I want is a firm answer . . . I am going to live in _____. When you tell me, then I can arrange to have everything sent to you. I can't do anything now.

Things are almost back to normal, but haven't heard anything about the return of dependents yet. I'm sorry for the way this letter started off. I should have ripped the darn thing up and started all over again. Please let me know as soon as possible what you decide to do.   Love, Bill

*

5 November, 1962

Dearest Patsy,

Just got your letter of the 31st. The express shipment will go this week to your folks home for the lack of a better address.

Don't know what happened to all of the letters I've sent. One went to my folks home. The rest were sent to Briggs. One of them is most important since it has a check for $100 in it.

Things are slowing down and are just about normal, if that is the word for it. Still haven't had a day off yet. Say hello to your folks for me. Give the kids a big hug for me. Will write soon again.   Love, Bill

16-1 The residential Gitmo community was converted to a war machine over night ... shown here is one of the bunkers built into the hillside above the Base Chapel

16-2

Marine Commander, Colonel George W. Killen, with some of his troops

17

Home is Where . . .?

We remained with the Kuchler family for over a week, by which time my children had partially recovered from their severe colds. We were generously housed in a large room of our own, with one bed for me, and another for the two children. Our host family showered us with hospitality and love, making us feel as if we were doing them a favor by staying with them.

The day after our arrival, Trudy and I were having a cup of tea downstairs when I heard Colleen awaken from her nap. When I came up to the bedroom, I discovered Billy still sound asleep with an empty medicine bottle clutched in his hand. I had been giving one children's Coricidin tablet to each child every four hours for their nasal congestion. Living out of a suitcase in unfamiliar circumstances, I had taken this bottle out of my luggage and left it on a bedside table.

Trudy went into action, driving Billy and me to the Naval Hospital without delay. The Kuchler children agreed to take care of Colleen while we were gone. Not long after our arrival, the doctor came out and took Billy from my arms. As I started to follow, he insisted I remain where I was. He had apparently experienced one too many agitated mothers witnessing the pumping of their child's stomach.

Within about 45 minutes, the doctor carried my limp son out saying, "He's had all the Marine pumped out of him."
He then told Trudy and me we would have to remain around the hospital for the rest of the day, keeping Billy

walking as much as possible. By 5 p.m., the doctor pronounced him well enough to be released.

Not too many days after our arrival in Norfolk, I began to hear rumblings from the service grapevine that evacuees would be provided air transportation out of the area to anywhere in the United States they wished, even as far away as Hawaii. In contrast, some were electing to stay in barracks at Little Creek in case return might be imminent. Chick Killen was among them. I also learned that even if I wanted to be first in line for return to Gitmo, it had not yet been determined whether returning was even an option.

Should I stay in Norfolk in the hope of a decision to return? If I decided to stay, how would we be housed, and for how long? Would relocation elsewhere, even temporarily, jeopardize my chances for return? It became clear that no one was able to answer these questions for me, and I was feeling pressure to do *something*. At this juncture in our exodus, I was exhausted. All I wanted was to go 'home', and I didn't even know where that was.

I felt an urgent need to create a sense of sanctuary for my equally confused and travel-weary children, but coupled with my exhaustion, the profusion of unknowns was paralyzing. There were also other people to consider. How could I justify not accepting the hospitality of my in-laws? How could I refuse the kindness of my husband's cousin in Norfolk? And, how could I explain to him my ambivalence about staying close to the military community?

Near the end of his speech to the nation on October 22, 1962, President Kennedy said, "The cost of freedom is always high . . . but Americans have always paid it." Where did my <u>personal</u> freedom enter into this equation? What control did I have over my life when the gangplank was raised on the *Upshur*? Being expected to surrender my personal freedom and allow myself to be carried along by circumstances seemed to render me incapable of reclaiming control over my life. Lacking confidence about my ability to make a good decision, I delayed making any decision. I was certain even my children saw through my delaying tactics and realized how scared I was.

Faced with continued uncertainty and fear, I turned to my usual resource. Through prayer, I knew emotionally that, to me, home meant family. I made the decision to return to the home of my parents in Salt Lake City, Utah.

In an effort to make the trip as streamlined as possible, the Marine Corps travel personnel arranged for a lay-over in Chicago O'Hare Airport with as little time between planes as possible. But being accustomed to dealing with combat-ready Marines, they had no experience with estimating how long it might take for a woman encumbered with two toddlers to get between terminals. To compound the problem, our arrival on the ground in O'Hare was late. Near panic, I grabbed a baggage cart, and put Billy in the top basket. I then plopped the carry-on bag in his lap, draping our coats across it. I lifted Colleen onto the extension below and told her to hang onto the basket. Running as fast as I could maneuver my cargo through the crowded corridors, we arrived at our gate as they were announcing the final call.

Still on liquid penicillin for his ear infection, Billy's system rejected the pink medicine somewhere over Nebraska. Luckily, I had brought a change of clothing for him in the carry-on bag. When he had a repeat occurrence over Colorado, he was stuck with returning to Utah in a somewhat shopworn condition.

Billy finally fell asleep in my arms shortly before landing, and Colleen was asleep in the seat with her head resting against my hip. As we touched down on the tarmac, I was filled with relief that our exodus might be over and I could unpack the bags at last.

We taxied slowly to our gate, whereupon as soon as the engines cut off, the intercom piped in the soothing voice of Perry Como. People averted their eyes as they filed past us, and I could see my father and brother frantically circling the plane on the tarmac after they realized all the other passengers had disembarked, but I was simply sobbing too deeply to move as Perry Como continued to croon, "Everybody Has a Home but Me."

17-1

Host and hostess of the author during her stay in the Norfolk area ... Chief Warrant Officer Lester W. Kuchler and his wife, Trudy, at their home in Portsmouth, Virginia

17-2 Children of the Kuchler family... Lester, Jr., Gertrude, and Betty

18

Life in the Interim

Comforting as it was to get 'home', incorporating three additional people into my parent's house resulted in crowded conditions. My 22-year-old brother, Jack, was also still living at home. And, more than the crowded conditions was concern about the unknown.

The Cuban Missile Crisis ensued with no known end in sight. I realized my parents were nearly as emotionally affected as was I. This traumatic upheaval was not happening out there somewhere in the world called Cuba. It was affecting their one and only daughter as well as the tender psyches of their only grandchildren. How long would our future remain unsettled?

> 12 November 1962
> Guantanamo Bay, Cuba

Dearest Patsy,

Haven't heard a thing about length of tour or return of dependents. As I see it now, dependents won't be returned here until this business with Castro is really finished. I know they won't be returned as long as we have the troop concentration here. As for tour length, nothing official has come out on that.

Last night I went up to the Club for dinner. Met a few of the newsmen who are in here to cover GTMO ... Brien Duff from the Copley papers, Mr. Medici from Italy and Tim Creery from Canada. At first, GTMO was the only subject, but the conversation then switched to other topics like literary styles of various authors, newspaper reporting ethics, and so forth. Don't know when I've enjoyed a conversation more. Such a change from the conversations we've had around here lately.

Your letters sure keep me off balance. Every time I think I have it all set up, I get another letter from you changing the whole thing. I don't think we should pay the price differential for a furnished apartment when we can easily get our own stuff from North Carolina. Going to have to buy two tires for the car before I ship it.

Work has been going on much the same until this morning. Was given three big reporting deadlines and will have to work nights to meet them. One good thing about the workload is it doesn't give me much time to think.

See ya later, kid. Sure miss not having you hanging around. Hug the kids for me and give my regards to everyone. Will write soon again.   I love you, Bill

*

Compounded by the crowding and the unknown was my parents complete incomprehension of my hope of returning to Cuba. They were not alone in this. Friends, other relatives, and neighbors would all be unable to keep from blurting out, "But why would you want to go back?" To which my automatic reply would always be, "It's my home!" I was in denial that anything had changed, moving through each day as if sleep-walking, anticipating the moment of return and coming to life again where I had left off.

Even in my dazed condition, there was only so long I could tolerate living out of a suitcase. My mental health demanded moving forward with some more stable arrangement. Having no other alternative, I had to assume our relocation might be extended, so I began looking for rental units in the neighborhood where I grew up knowing this would give me the greatest feeling of security. I had to impose upon my father's help for this endeavor, as I had no means of transportation, and Salt Lake is not public-transportation friendly. My mother became the willing babysitter during these excursions. Luckily my children were not yet school age, so that situation didn't enter into the equation. With my father's help, I found a walk-in apartment in a familiar neighborhood.

The necessity of a first and last payment made me acutely aware of my economic situation. With a loan from my parents, I opened a local bank account.

14 November 1962

Dearest Patsy,

My packers will put all the stuff in a box probably tomorrow and have the shipment on its way. Enclosing copy of the letter I sent to North Carolina to get our furniture out of storage. Don't know how long it will take for you to finish the paper work and get it.

Back to work. This office is hotter than the devil. Air conditioner broke down. Give the kids a hug for me, and my regards to all concerned. Miss ya, kid.   I love you, Bill

*

We had stored our furniture in Camp Lejeune, North Carolina when we had left for Cuba. In order to get it out of storage in a military facility, I was required to go through the official military channels, none of which recognized me as a separate entity from my Marine husband. I had to complete the paperwork at a local Military installation, and have it mailed back to my husband for signature before it could be shipped to me in Salt Lake, now that I finally had an address.

None of the usual lines of communication were in operation at Gitmo, and our attempts at correspondence had proved entirely unsatisfactory. Either our letters crossed in the mail or became impossibly delayed, which introduced misunderstanding and frustration into an already unworkable situation. The official permission to ship our furniture dragged on. While waiting for it to arrive, my father began helping me clean, fix, and paint the apartment to make it more agreeable to my taste.

19 November 1962

Dearest Patsy,

Finally got the household stuff packed for shipment. Hope to have it on the ship leaving here Friday. Also hope to have the car on the same boat. Will write Les Kuchler in Norfolk to let him know it's on the way and also ask him to get two tires for it since I can't get any whitewalls here. Will advise you when it actually leaves. Please send Les a blank check for the tires.

Flaps come and flaps go down here. A minor one is now in the wind. Think it is connected with the President's speech tomorrow night. All of the air conditioners went out in the office today and it is hotter than blue blazes in here!

After this money bit is settled, I'll probably send you the entire check for deposit. That sure will be a nice windfall. Got to get back to work. Say hello to everyone for me. And don't forget to hug the kids for me. Keep your chin up, Buddy. This won't be forever.   I love you, Bill

*

During all this strife, I was fortunate my parents were flexible. They had been suffering from three years of long-distance grandparenting. We lived across the country in Jacksonville, North Carolina when the children were born, and other than brief visits, they had no hands-on experience with their only grandchildren. This was their chance to make up for it. We took frequent excursions to parks, and the zoo, and enjoyed visits to friends and relatives, during which they made it obvious how much it pleased them to have their grandchildren with them.

My father rigged a 'roller-coaster' in his back yard. He nailed together a wheeled contraption that exactly fit the metal tracks. This car could accommodate one of my children at a time. It picked up a bit of momentum as it rolled along the tracks, and under his careful supervision, Billy and Colleen could take turns riding along the gently sloping rails with Grandpa providing the momentum in troughs.

Positioned by the picture window in the front room of my parent's home was a large, overstuffed rocking chair. Daddy would often be in it with both children on his lap, gently rocking them and singing one of the nonsense songs I remembered from my childhood . . .
"All around the chicken coop,
The possum chased the weasel.
That's the way the money goes,
Pop goes the weasel."
At the word 'pop', his legs would suddenly open and threaten to drop the children to the floor. They **loved** it! The warm sun was streaming through the window when I returned from an errand one afternoon and came upon all three of them sound asleep in the rocker.

*

20 November 1962

Hey Buddy,

These one-sided conversations are the pits. Have to take the car down this morning and have it booked for the ship leaving Friday. Can't find the plates to put on it. Will probably have to register the car all over again. They were in the garage last time I looked. Oh well!

Eager to hear what the President will have to say tonight. I'm sure the reporters will have some very pointed questions for him. Reporters from the "Leatherneck" magazine were down here the past few weeks doing a story. It should be published in February. Will try to get a copy to send to you. I think they will at least mention the mobile clothing store I set up. It seems to be working out well.

The men down here are still holding out hope that dependents will be returned. The way I see it we have to get rid of the bearded one first. Sure hope we get around to it. This thing will never be settled by talking.

Get the kids an ice cream cone for me. Miss you more than you will ever realize. Will try to put a letter in the mail tomorrow.   I love you, Bill

*

Article from Leatherneck Magazine – February 1963

The Marine Barracks has a self-contained supply section. During the first days of the emergency it was the only Marine supply agency on the base. "Every Marine unit that arrived called on us for gear," reports Captain William F. Kendig, the Barracks Supply Officer. "The first few days were hectic, but we managed to take care of everyone."

Boondocking has always been hard on utilities and boots, so it wasn't long before Captain Kendig's clothing sales store was swamped with Marines looking for replacement uniforms. Because only a few of the infantrymen could leave the defense line at any one time, it was almost impossible for some of the men to get new uniforms when they needed them. The Marine Barracks supply men solved that problem. They borrowed two trucks from the

109

Navy, filled them with uniform items, installed a cash register, and sent the 'store' up to the troops.

*

In his speech on November 20, 1962, President Kennedy announced that he had instructed the Secretary of Defense to lift the Naval quarantine. He reported to the American people real progress had been made thus far in fulfilling understandings between himself and Soviet Chairman Khrushchev. While he said the U.S. would not abandon the political, or economic efforts to halt subversion from Cuba, these policies were very different from any intent to launch a military invasion of the island.

*

During the lulls between apartment hunting and renovation, there were excursions to one park or another, where my Dad would push his grandchildren on the swings, run along side the round-de-go, and jump on with them for a ride, or let them feed the ducks. One excursion proved especially exciting.

Dad used to bring stale popcorn home from the Elks Club on Bingo nights and store it in his garage to feed the birds. On a particular sunny afternoon, he threw two of these bags in the trunk of his car so we'd have something to feed the ducks. At the park, he handed one of these bags to each of the kids. Billy's bag immediately came to life. It bounced and swayed and nearly jostled out of his hand until a mouse emerged from the bottom of it, trailing popcorn from the hole it had created as an escape route. It would be hard to guess who was more surprised . . . the mouse or Billy.

110

18-1　Cover of Leatherneck Magazine containing article
about activities of Captain Kendig

Fortunately, the Marine Barracks has a self-contained supply section. During the first days of the emergency it was the only Marine supply agency on the base. "Every Marine unit that arrived called on us for gear," reports Captain William F. Kendig, the Barracks supply officer. "The first few days were hectic, but we managed to take care of everyone."

18-2   At the park in Salt Lake … author's mother, Larene Hale; brother, Jack holding Billy/Colleen; and author's father, John C. Hale

18-3 Improvised roller coaster in Hale backyard with
Grandpa Hale serving as locomotion

19

Yes, Virginia, There is a Santa Claus

The other Marine officer's wives and I continued to keep in touch when possible. Claire sent me the following letter:

November 14, 1962

Dear Pat and Chillun,

I, too went through a period of feeling like the situation was all <u>around</u> me without <u>involving</u> me. I guess I didn't realize just how noticeable it was until I was leaving Houston, and Grandpa said,
"Well, I'm glad to see you've decided to come down to earth and <u>do</u> something!"

It was a real toss-up between my staying in Houston, and being near my sister and her children (who are Kay, Beth, and Frank's ages), or living in Austin near my Daddy, and where <u>I</u> had friends. As soon as I got to Austin, I knew it was home.

Ken's letters have not given me too much hope of our getting back to Gitmo anytime soon, but I was relieved to know that the horses had all been bought by Special Services, and that we were not being charged for quarters in Gitmo as of the 22nd of October . . . day we left. At least we're not paying double housing!

I surely have appreciated having our car here for use. It does things for my state of independence!! Better close and go pick the kids up at school. Keep in touch.   Fondly, Claire

*

I also heard from Chick Killen from the Marine Barracks in Portsmouth, Virginia:

November 18, 1962

Dearest Pat:

Just delighted to hear from you. Your new little 'temporary' home sounds ideal for you and the kiddies. Know how relieved Bill must feel knowing you are comfortably situated near your parents. I'm sure after much consideration, you made the wise decision to return to Salt Lake!

We are getting along fine. The boys are in good schools and seem to be adjusting nicely. George's letters seem to come in bunches . . . none for many days, then several. He writes, "These are hectic days".
Don't we know it!

He feels it will be some time before families can return to Gitmo, and one large drawback would be reestablishing the schools. However, let none of us give up hope of returning. Hope it won't be too long. As mentioned before, should I receive any kind of encouraging news, will get in touch immediately, and you do the same.

George sent us 6 boxes recently, so we are warm again. Thanks for the negatives. Will return them soon and answer your nice letter at the same time, but for now, you and those darling kiddos have a nice Thanksgiving.   Fondly, Chick

*

115

The letters from my husband held out hope that someday the things he had promised to send would actually reach me:

25 November 1962

Dearest Patsy,

Am still working on the shipments of household gear to you. And will let you know when the car has actually left for Norfolk.

Cal told me that Karen is pregnant again. And Patrick Collins has been told by Mary that the doctor thinks she is carrying twins. Must have been something in the water down here!

Last night for some reason the separation really got to me. Never felt so low in all my life. Maybe it was because it's the first time I've permitted myself to think about it. This too shall pass!

Hope you and the kids are doing well. Bet you will really have a ball putting the new place together. Well, honey, give the kids a big hug and kiss for me. As for you, I'll do that myself mentally. I love you, Bill ---miss you too much to say!

*

The days sloughed by, and evolved into weeks. Without too much effort, the weeks turned into months, and still the children and I were not settled in a place of our own. The thing that kept this unsettled time from becoming intolerable was the constancy of the love and support in which we were enveloped.

Looking back at the snapshots of our Thanksgiving feast, I realize it was a celebration of being fed with other than food. I don't know how I would have survived this period without family.

27 November 1962
Gitmo

Dear Patsy,

How's the world treating you? Admiral O'Donnell sent out the following dispatch for Thanksgiving that I thought was rather good:

For all hands at Guantanamo, this is a most significant Thanksgiving. We are here, separated from our families, maintaining a position of readiness which has already made a vital contribution to the security and well being of our country. All of us have many reasons to be thankful on this traditional day, but high on the list for everyone here should be thanks for the honor of being entrusted with the task of defending this base, and with it, the cause of all free peoples of the Western hemisphere. "

The only thing that remains unsettled is when do you return here. CNO *[Chief of Naval Operations]* is now asking for planning purposes how many will want to return, how long it will take them to get to Norfolk and where they are right now. This request is just making it harder to determine whether I should ship anything more home or if I should keep it here.

I'm not holding out hope for immediate return. Think it's better to go the other way and send everything. We can always have it sent back when the time comes. Can't be disappointed if you plan for the worst.

Bought a new record album yesterday . . . Glenn Miller . . . is the name of it. Really great! The Colonel bought one too. We listened to it last night at his house. Tonight, he and I are going to do a little bowling. He has never done any, but I don't think it will take him too long to pick it up. The Command Bowling League is starting again and I'll be bowling in it. Will get a refund for the Mixed League.

Give the kids a hug and a kiss for me. I'll bang out another note as soon as I can.   I love you, Bill

*

30 November 1962

Dearest Patsy,

How is the world treating you today? Has any of the stuff shown up yet? This place is beginning to settle down and things are getting back to normal. One of the augmenting forces is leaving today . . . a good sign.

Right now, it's hard to say just when you will return. There are still a few problems remaining to be solved . . . schools, travel, and the like. Here the Navy is working on it and has asked everyone to state if their families are willing to return and how long it will take them to get to a point of embarkation. I told them it would take you two days. If you came by air, it would be no problem.

With the car, just reverse the procedure. In regard to household effects and furniture, contact the reserve company to have the necessary forms prepared. If I get the orders, I'll airmail them to you. If you get them direct, (and I think you will) just take them with you when you have the forms made up.

At this end, I don't see any real problems. When the call comes, you can have your family handle the mopping up operations. All you have to do now is to plan ahead, make your packing lists, alert your family, and don't sign a lease for the apartment.

This sounds very optimistic I know, and I usually don't plan this way, but I just don't want you to be caught short. Rumors are a dime a dozen here, and no one knows which way to go. All I know is the Navy is making plans for return of dependents, though no definite date has been established. Sure wish I knew more.

Is it true you fed the kids two pounds of popcorn? You said you took them to the park and they had two pounds of popcorn. Don't think that's a good diet, do you?

Work remains pretty much the same except I'm writing a hell of a lot of letters to Commandant of the Marine Corps for one thing or another. Got to rush. Have a few things that can't be put off. Will try to write again tomorrow. Give the kids a hug for me.   Love, Bill

*

3 December 1962

Hi honey,

Just a note to let you know I'm still around. Don't know what shipments went when. Do know they are gone. Packers were by themselves with my list. The house is mine. The Colonel wants us in the houses so no one can move into them.

Saw an AP wire picture of a woman in a wool suit with a straw hat! What do you think of that? Trying to get a glossy print of it.

Things are pretty much the same. Work, eat, sleep. Funny. Didn't like the single life when I had it, and here I am again! Now I like it even less. No fun at all. Kiss the kids for me. Yo te amo, Bill

*

7 December 1962

Dearest Patsy,

Sorry didn't get to write sooner, but as you know, we are in the middle of another 'flap'. All of the people sent down here are now making preparations to return to the States. I'm trying to recapture as many of the express shipments as possible, get quarters renovated for new people to come here, put the barracks back into shape so we can get our people in from the field, straighten out the account and gosh knows what else. Needless to say, I'm busy.

As of this writing, I know nothing of the arrangements being made for your return. All I know is that some of the wives are coming in today by plane from Norfolk. We have seen nothing official as to when or how everyone is coming back. I do know one ship will be leaving New York on the 11th and will make a second trip on the 19th. Perhaps you'll be on it! In any case, you should have something official soon. I hear they expect to have approximately 1800 dependents back here by the 22nd of this month.

Do hope you were able to contact Kuchler and have the car stopped at Norfolk. With no plates, should have slowed him up enough not to have handed it over yet.

Our household effects went out on the ship leaving the same day they announced the return of dependents. The Shipping Officer told me yesterday there would be no problem getting the stuff back here again. I will take steps to have the shipment of furniture from Lejeune rerouted here as soon as I can get some kind of authority to do so. In any case, don't let them unpack the stuff. We'll just get it here and I can leave it packed and in storage. .

Sure hope you make it by Christmas. Got to get back to work. Hope this letter doesn't reach you in Salt Lake, but rather that it comes back to GTMO.   Love, Bill

*

When the phone rang on December 6th, the woman on the other end of the line said, "This is Western Union calling for Mrs. Patricia H. Kendig".
"This is she," I managed to stammer out.
Then she read me the following message from the Bureau of Naval Personnel in Washington, D.C.:

Travel instructions: You and your children, if any, report to Naval Representative at the North Lounge, Pier 4, Brooklyn Army Terminal, 58th and First Avenue, Brooklyn, New York, between 9:00 am and 11:00 am, 19 Dec. 1962 for passage to Guantanamo via the USNS Geiger. Present this message as authority for passage. Should you reject this offer of passage, promptly telephone collect at Oxford 41495, Washington, D.C. If transportation to New York needed, present this message to nearest Naval activity who are hereby authorized to issue Transportation Request for required travel.
Merry Christmas.

It is difficult to convey my feelings. I jumped up and exploded in tears, not hardly believing that my wildest dreams had come true. This was the first real emotional breakdown I'd allowed myself, and it took awhile to calm myself enough to let my parents know the nature of the call and the reason for my tears.

The local telegraph office delivered a copy of their message within the hour. After it arrived, I phoned in a telegram to my husband telling him the good news. When I told the operator it was to be sent to Guantanamo Bay, Cuba, she said,
"How do you spell that?"
At this, I nearly laughed out loud. The Cuban Missile Crisis and Guantanamo Bay, Cuba had been my total focus for so long, I found it impossible to comprehend there was anyone in the world who didn't know how to spell Guantanamo. It made me feel like a foreigner in my native land.

After I had given the operator the spelling, she said,
"You have one more word. Would you like to add 'love'?"
I answered, "No. He <u>knows</u> I love him. Add <u>Hallelujah!</u>
There was a long pause, after which she said,
"How do you spell that?"

Family Receives Best Gift, Christmas At Guantanamo

19-1   Photo of author and her children that appeared in one
of the Salt Lake papers announcing their return to Cuba

WESTERN UNION
TELEGRAM
W. P. MARSHALL, PRESIDENT

SP-1201 (4-60)

The filing time shown in the date line on domestic telegrams is LOCAL TIME at point of origin. Time of receipt is LOCAL TIME at point of destination

```
S22A PST DEC 6 62 LA199
L OGAO45 DL GOVT PD WUX HILL AIR FORCE BASE UTAH 6 1005A MST
MRS PATRICIA L KENDIG
   1267 SHERMAN AVE SALT LAKE CITY UTAH
UNCLAS .
      TRAVEL INSTRUCTIONS.
                                       AL
      YOU AND YOUR CHILDREN, IF ANY, REPORT TO NAVY REPRESENTATIVE
AT THE NORTH LOUNGE, PIER 4, BROOKLYN ARMY TERMINAL, 58TH AND
FIRST AVENUE, BROOKLYN, NEW YORK, BETWEEN 9:00 AM AND 11:00AM,
19 DEC 1962 FOR PASSAGE TO GUANTANAMO VIA THE USNS GEIGER.
PRESENT THIS MESSAGE AS AUTHORITY FOR PASSAGE. SHOULD YOU REJECT
THIS OFFER OF PASSAGE, PROMPTLY TELEPHONE COLLECT AT OXFORD
41595, WASHINGTON, D.C. IF ASSISTANCE REQUIRED UPON ARRIVAL
                Shorebroad
NEW YORK, CALL SHORERCAD 5-6044. TRANSPORTATION CHARGEABLE
TO APPOPRIATION 1731453.2218 22/33600 EA 74330. COST OF TRAVEL
MAY BE CLAIMED ON ARRIVAL GTMO BUT IF TRANSPORTATION TO NEW
```

19-2   Copy of the actual telegram author received from Bureau of Naval Personnel, Washington D.C. on December 6, 1962, approving return to Guantanamo Bay

20

Deja Vu

Although time seemed to move like molasses onboard ship, while staying with the Kuchlers' in Norfolk, and living with my folks in Salt Lake, from the day I received the telegram granting me permission to return, it was put on fast-forward. The long-awaited shipments began arriving in Salt Lake, and I was inundated with paperwork to reverse the process. I was able to get out of the lease for our prospective apartment, but the energy and money that went into preparing it for occupancy was a total loss.

The local newspaper, *The Deseret News and Telegram,* came to my parents' home to interview me and photograph the children and me with our luggage. This article and picture were published on December 13, 1962. According to a front- page story in that same newspaper, there were two Navy families, one in Nephi, Utah and one in Yuma, Arizona, who flew back to Gitmo. Apparently we were the only Gitmo 'evacuees' in Salt Lake City.

I received a telegram from my husband on December 7th asking that I notify Kuchlers' (the dear family who housed us in Norfolk) to claim the car and have it returned to Cuba. From the Kuchlers', I learned our car, household goods, clothes, and Christmas gifts on a ship bound for Norfolk had been 'recaptured' in mid-ocean and were being returned to Cuba.

After contact with local Naval personnel, I arranged transportation on a flight to Brooklyn, New York, where my husband's parents would meet us and take us to their home in New Jersey for the night. They would then drive us back to Brooklyn the next day for our 9 am departure by ship for the final leg of our journey to Cuba.

Salt Lake City, Utah lies is a valley between the Wasatch and Oquirrh mountain ranges. Picturesque as this might be most of the year, during the winter the combination of pollution and weather conditions often produces what is known as an inversion. It causes a thick, gray cloud to hover low over the valley, completely obscuring the sun for as long as two months. The only thing capable of dispersing an inversion is heavy precipitation accompanied by high winds.

In keeping with the little gray cloud of disaster that seemed to have haunted us for the last several months, the inversion arrived December 14th. We were due to fly out December 18th. The airport was closed, as visibility through the cloud cover was nil.

When the inversion showed no sign of lifting, and there were no predictions of any corrective weather fronts moving into the area within the foreseeable future, I made a command decision. We took a train from Salt Lake on December 16th for the overnight trip to Denver, Colorado, where my cousin, Jacqueline Kammer, husband Paul, and their family met us and took us to their home for the night of December 17th.

The morning of December 18th, Jacqueline and her family put us on the flight that had been unable to land in Salt Lake because of the inversion, thus allowing us to keep our Brooklyn rendezvous with my husband's parents. In a letter to their son, his parents told him,
"I guess you picked the right kind of wife for your career. Pat wasn't crying on anybody's shoulder. She said, 'it all goes with the Military life.'"

We boarded the USNS *Geiger* at Brooklyn Naval Yard on December 19th for the last leg of our journey *home,* and psychologically, during this entire indefinite period, it had remained *'home'*. I had never lost my resolve to return to Gitmo!

The return trip aboard the *Geiger* was luxurious. We had a private stateroom with two bunk beds and an adjoining bathroom with shower, toilet, and washbasin. I took the top bunk, settling the children in the bottom one.   Through all of this, they had remained unbelievably resilient and agreeable, especially now that they were both well.

Meals were announced with a lovely chime. We drew first seating, where place cards indicated our seating. By the second meal, the attending steward knew my beverage of choice was hot tea, and had it waiting at my place.

Unlike the dearth of news on our last voyage, there was a daily paper, *"The Geiger Counter"*, which included a recap of national and international news. Somewhere out at sea, we crossed the time line that meant we had lost two hours. The *Geiger Counter* acknowledged this event with the following notice:
Lost
Somewhere between sunrise and sunset,
Two golden hours,
Set with 60 diamond minutes each,
No reward . . . just lost forever.
It was clear to me that wasn't all that was lost in this passage! Lost was the constant uncertainty, fear, and stress that had permeated the previous two months.

The morning of Saturday, December 22nd was cloudless. The brilliance of the sun reflected off waves that changed from azure to aqua as the large ship nosed through them. My children and I were on deck, reveling in the warmth and beauty, breathing deeply of the salty air.   It all felt reminiscent of those few idyllic months before the evacuation. Raising my head, I looked up at the sky, and said aloud, "Thank you, Lord!"

Before we could even see land, we heard the jets crossing high over our ship. Then we saw the tugs steaming toward us almost in procession. When they reached our ship, they turned and began their escort operation, but more than that, they were spouting jets of red, white, and green water ahead of us. Helicopters arrived, hovering close overhead, and began dropping streamers out of their doors onto our deck. Above them all, the jets continued their thunderous welcome, leaving contrails of white scrolls in their wake.

While distracted by all this, land loomed into view, and the sound of music wafted across the water. As we got closer, we could see the crowds waving, hear the cheers and the bands, and see the banners raised high in greeting. This time I entered enthusiastically into the celebratory spirit. The stimulation of it was almost more than I could bear, coupled with the knowledge that among the greeters was the one I had been yearning to see for these two long and arduous months.

We stood on deck waiting for the docking and lowering of the gangplank. I shaded my eyes and kept looking for Bill. It was difficult to make out faces at that distance, but the largest banner was red and gold and I could clearly read its message:
Welcome Marine Wives
My heart almost burst with joy when I saw this, and I was unable to stop the tears. I was soon openly sobbing without any restraint or embarrassment, finally letting loose those pent up emotions kept two months inside. It was as if I knew it was ok to give vent to them now because the ordeal was finally over. We had arrived. **We were home!**

21

Return to Paradise

During the first few months of 1963, I was so full of joy at being back in Gitmo that I didn't dwell on the constant reminders that things were not exactly normal. Being reunited with my husband and beloved friends touched me to the core. The emotional bond between us seemed especially poignant because of the life-threatening experience we had shared.

When I was able to examine our predicament from a practical point of view, disturbing questions surfaced. Would our children be safe? How could we pretend to create the semblance of a peaceful home in what still remained a war zone? And, how could we resume our previous life when it was obvious nothing was the same?

Unable to deal with these issues when I first returned, I sublimated them, and went into some kind of a trance. I do remember clinging so tightly to my husband after I had walked down the gangplank that he had difficulty extracting himself from my grip. I needed to convince myself he was flesh and bone and this was not yet another dream.

The extravagance of this welcome continued as we walked into our home, but I have no recollection of it. Luckily we have pictorial proof. All of our own ornaments and lights had arrived the previous day, but my husband had not trusted this would happen, so he had purchased new decorations. Not knowing what else to do when our own trimmings were returned, he added them to the tree, so it was absolutely laden down with garnishment. And at the bottom of this glut of glitter lay a sumptuous mound of wrapped gifts. No wonder I was thrown into a trance.

In my dazed condition, the ensuing days felt enchanted. My eurphoria at being reunited as a family affected even the most mundane activities. Picking limes from our backyard made me giddy. Drinking in the glistening waters of the Guantanamo Bay was such a heady experience I thought I might faint. And I could not contain my tears of joy the first time I climbed aboard Tibbs and reveled in the pungent smell of the horse trails. On my first trip back to Kittery Beach, I wanted to run and shout and enfold the scene within me so it would never disappear again. Even the commissary and PX took on a rose-colored hue.

Each new day seemed like a gift. I savored the gentle call of the morning dove, and reveled in the lushness of the tropical flowers. After hearing that my family in Utah was blanketed in snow, picking avocados, tomatoes, limes, and bananas from my backyard filled me with awe. It seemed like almost too much of a good thing. The ambiance thrilled me more than when I had first arrived.

There was, however, no doubt that during October of 1962, our pleasant 'hometown' had been converted into a fortress. Many signs of fortification still remained. The bunkers that lined the hill below the chapel served as a constant reminder that a serious episode in history had been played out here. Huge strips of black tape in the shape of a 'V' were securely affixed to our front and back doors as the signal to the evacuation team that all dependents in the house had left. Paper was still pealing off our car headlights as remnants of the complete blackout.

Late one afternoon, I heard a low rumbling and felt an unusual vibration. My children and I searched for the source of this phenomenon. At the juncture of Marine Point with the main thoroughfare of Sherman Avenue, we encountered six large tanks slowly rumbling down the road on their way from one place to another. While we were watching, one of the tanks threw a cleat, and they all had to stop while the disabled tank got back on track. It was a time-consuming process. My neighbors and I had time to stroll to our quarters and return with lawn chairs and cold drinks to help us enjoy this impromptu parade.

In another instance, we were ordered inside our homes for several hours when a tank on the hill above us turned on its side with its loaded guns aimed directly at our housing complex. And, I was jolted back to the nightmare of October 22nd by the following notice in the Gitmo Gazette:

If you are missing a footlocker shipped on evacuation, contact Mr. Wilkinson at Ext. 8495. It contains ladies clothing and other items.[1]

Not only in our community but internationally the debris of the Crisis continued, as reported in the following news item:

The New York Times news service, in a Washington dispatch, said 560 Soviet servicemen sailed from Havana last Saturday on the Russian liner Gruzia, an 11,030-ton Black Sea cruiser ship.[2]

As a follow up to this item, sources said the President was drafting a personal message to Soviet Premier Nikita Khrushchev prodding him to speed up the troop pullout. He told a news conference that although 4,500 Soviet combat troops had left Cuba since the October crisis, a total of 17,000 Russian military personnel and technicians still remained early in 1963. This knowledge would have unnerved me had I allowed myself to dwell on it.

Reminders of how the Cuban people were continuing to be affected by the October Crisis were also prevalent:

Miami – Some 14,000 Cubans have fled Fidel Castro's Communist regime in small boats and 1,000 others who took this risky escape route died in the attempt, the Cuban Human Rights Commission says. [3]

We had a Cuban maid (Sobeida) who was an 'exile' (unable to return to the Cuba mainland). She lived in her own quarters over our garage. I commented one day on her new shoes. She usually went barefoot or wore only rubber flip-flops. She told me they belonged to her friend who had bought them at the Post Exchange for her daughter. Sobeida was wearing them to make them look old so her friend (who was not an exile) could carry them out the gate past the Cuban militiamen. They could not carry out anything purchased on the Base.

Additionally, intermittent strip-down searches were conducted by Cuban guards at the gate to see that the Cubans employed on the Base weren't carrying out anything unauthorized. Chick Killen, gave her maid some fabric. The woman sewed herself a skirt out of these yard goods, and ask Chick for enough rice to fill the hem for her starving children (she had eight). Even if the indigenous workers had the money, there was simply no food available for purchase in Cuba. The maid wore the hand-made skirt out the gate that evening, and Chick worried and wondered whether she would ever see her again. Happily, that evening was not an occasion for strip-down searches, and the maid returned the next day.

One day after a morning at the pool, I took my children into the snack bar near the officer's club for lunch. Juan, who operated the cash register, traveled back and forth between Cuba proper and the Base daily. I mentioned that he looked tired. Covering a yawn with his hand, he told me how Castro's militiamen had broken into the family home in the middle of the night and rummaged under the bedding with the butt ends of their rifles to see if the family was hiding anything worth confiscating. They found nothing under the bedcovers, so went away with the family's television.

The following item published in the Gitmo Gazette was one of the most startling reminders that the Base had been converted into a war zone and had not yet recovered from this transition:

All base personnel are reminded that red triangular mine field warning signs are posted along the perimeter of danger areas for the obvious purpose of WARNING. There have been numerous reports in recent months of misguided individuals taking these red triangles for souvenirs. Replacement of them is a constant problem. Not only does this create extra work for security personnel, but creates an unnecessary hazard to life and limb. The message we are trying to get across is this:
DON'T TOUCH THOSE COTTON-PICKIN' RED TRIANGLES...THEY AIN'T NO SOUVENIRS!!!!! [4]

As a distraction from dealing with the contradictions of our life, I volunteered to write for the base newspaper. My by-line column, entitled "Scene Around Gitmo", began appearing weekly. I gushed over the pampas grass, the beach, the weather, and even the indigenous bugs. Many of my articles reported information unique to our living conditions. Excerpts from some of these follow.

July 28, 1963 **Scene Around Gitmo** by Pat Kendig

Dr. R. J. Scrumenti, Dermitologist of the Naval Hospital, has been kind enough to share with me some information about the Mango and its poinsonous reaction. Mango poisoning is the second most prevalent cause of dermatoses on this Base. Dr. Scrimenti suggests that in order not to be lulled into a sense of false security, we treat the Mango tree and its fruit as if it were poison ivy.

If an individual in your family has a known sensitivity to poison ivy, he should not pick Mangoes, eat them, or even venture near the tree. The allergen from the Mango tree is contained within the sap, and since it is an allergy-producing tree, everyone should be very cautious about sampling the fruit.

The dermatitis resulting from contact with the sap of the Mango tree can be disabling. Many cases respond to drugs and the reaction can be short-lived. There have been cases, however, where individuals were unable to take the drugs and swelling and disability has continued for as long as a month.

Since the Mango tree is especially inviting as a climbing tree, parents are cautioned not to permit this. A child who may not have been exposed to this particular allergen before could escape dermatitis on first contact, but this does not mean immunity will continue.

September 21, 1963 – **Scene Around Gitmo** by Pat Kendig

It's a lovely lawn party, and between bites of hors d'oeuvres, guests are being eaten by the unseen enemy . . . the sand fly. Annoying as these pests may be, commonly known as 'flying teeth', they are not the Number One enemy of the Base Pest Control Department. The Number One culprit is the mosquito, whose bites may contain the potential for transmitting malaria fever. Because of this, control of the mosquito is the prime consideration of Mr. William E. Mayo and his hard-working staff.

Through a device known as the mosquito light trap, it has been established that the harmful anopheles Albimanus mosquito breeds on the Base. Before closing of the gate, this type mosquito was unknown on the Base. With Cuban permission, spray trucks from our Pest Control Department would drive into Guantanamo City and spray the area surrounding the base. Best information at present is that there is no pest control going on at all outside the gate of the Naval Base.

The Albimanus mosquito breeds best in contaminated water. Base residents are encouraged to throw all empty containers in covered garbage cans so they will not become water catchers and breeding places.

Although the sand fly is the next most common problem, this pest is only annoying and not harmful. A good coat of dirt keeps sand flies from coming through the screens of your homes, so advice from Pest Control is not to be too fastidious about cleaning your screens.

———————

September 28, 1963 **Scene Around Gitmo** by Pat Kendig

The great incidence of cockroaches on this Base is yet another of the problems encountered by the Pest Control Department. Hardly any home is without the cracks and crevices through which roaches gain entry from outside. Once inside, they reproduce so rapidly it is important to notify Pest Control as soon as you discover any in your quarters.

Spraying for roaches should be done no more often than every three months because these pests will build up a resistance with any more frequent spraying. All quarters are sprayed when vacant and then, upon request.

Next in importance is the termite.The drywood termite, a flying pest that travels in swarms, attacks wooden furniture and works of art. Similar damage is done by the powder post beetle, brought to our Base through the wooden products base residents purchase in Haiti. Residents are invited to bring wooden purchases to the Pest Control plant, where staff will run them through the fumigation chamber free of charge. It's a good idea to have all wooden products so treated, because waiting for evidence of pests in the wood results in a ruined product.

After listening to the challenges Mr. Mayo faces, I was surprised to learn he intends to extend his tour of duty here. The challenges in Gitmo present a unique professional training opportunity for him.

―――――

October 19, 1963 – **Scene Around Gitmo** by Pat Kendig

Along the road to the beach grow some lovely, wispy weeds. This time of year, they have gone to seed, and their fluffy lavender parachutes resemble heather. Shown off in your prettiest tall vase, they will last for weeks without water, providing you don't have two children who like to blow at them every time they pass to watch the seeds float around the house.

I stopped along the road to gather a bunch. No sooner had I turned off the ignition than a huge SeaBee dump truck came around a turn and stopped in front of my car. The young lad riding in the back asked what the problem was. Ordinarily at 9:30 in the morning, that beach road is deserted, but stop to pick a posey and . . . well, anyway, it was with a red face I was forced to tell him I was picking weeds.

Another time my love of nature nearly created an incident. Spotting a cactus plant in full bloom, I pulled off the road to take a picture. In pulling off the side of the road, I failed to notice a deep ditch, because it was concealed by weeds. After taking my photos, I was dismayed to discover that my right rear tire was completely suspended over this ditch, making friction, and therefore movement, impossible.

It was only minutes before a large Marine truck stopped. While he was investigating the situation, my neighbor, Colonel George W. Killen, recognizing our car, stopped to offer assistance. By the time our car was hauled from the small but significant precipice, my rescue squad included one fork lift truck, two $2^{1/2}$ ton trucks, one staff car and what appeared to be a Marine Battalion heading for a beach picnic.

Undaunted by either of these experiences, I continue to be a nature lover, and in Gitmo, have no difficulty finding material on which to lavish my affection. And aren't we lucky to be living in a community with zealous rescuers such as those from MCB-1 and the Marine Barracks.

---

[1] Gitmo Gazette – March 13, 1963
[2] Salt Lake Tribune – May 4, 1964
[3] Gitmo Gazette – January 7, 1963
[4] Gitmo Gazette – April 14, 1963

THE WHITE HOUSE
WASHINGTON

January 16, 1963

Dear Mrs. Kendig:

The President has asked me to convey to you
his warm thanks for your gracious letter and for
the sentiments which you express. He shares
your gratitude that the families at Guantanamo
could be reunited at Christmas and reciprocates
your good wishes for the New Year.

With the President's kind regards to you and
your family,

Sincerely,

Ralph A. Dungan
Special Assistant
to the President

Mrs. William F. Kendig
Navy No. 115, Box 22
c/o F.P.O.
New York, New York

21-1   Reply to letter of thanks author sent to President
Kennedy

21-2

Chick Killen, wife of Marine Commander, holding author's puppy with Margaret Gentry, daughter of Betty and Marine Intelligence Officer, Captain William R. Gentry

21-3   Colleen and Billy at their combined third and fourth birthday party ... actual dates of their birthdays are April 13 and 22

22

Flirtatious Flora

It seems ironic that Gitmo women and children endured not one, but three evacuations the year following our traumatic evacuation for the Cuban Missile Crisis. The first one was announced the evening of October 3rd as we were sitting down to dinner. The Base was in condition two-Bravo for Hurricane Flora, and my husband left the dinner table to report for duty. Not long thereafter, we heard his men outside nailing boards over the wooden louvers of our quarters.

I was in my seventh month of pregnancy, and with no air circulating through our rooms, I felt as if I was suffocating. In order to take my mind off this, I turned on a large fan and suggested to the children that we bake some blueberry muffins. I knew we had a prepackaged mix on hand that entailed merely adding milk and eggs. Their favorite step was loading the muffin tin with the papers and helping me spoon the mixture into them. Then, like magic, in very little time, the house was filled with a wonderful aroma, and out came the hot muffins.

We were each savoring a hot buttered muffin when we heard the three one-minute wails from the Base alarm system announcing Hurricane Condition Two-ALFA. This meant it had been determined Hurricane Flora could strike within four hours. According to **NAVBASE GTMO INSTRUCTION 3440.3D**, we were to proceed promptly by bus to our assigned shelter, since our quarters was not hurricane-proof.

When Condition Four had been declared earlier in the week, I had abided by instruction 3440.3D and packed our bags. I wasn't going to be unprepared a second time. I was in our bedroom, picking up our pre-packed bags, when my husband showed up.

"You're going to the underground hospital," he said.

"Why?" was my stunned reply.

"Because you're in your seventh month of pregnancy."

So instead of boarding the buses with the other Marine families, Bill drove me to the appointed place, where we followed the directions of the sentry.

My children and I spent the night in an underground bunker with other woman in their 7th through 9th month of pregnancy, or those women with infants 3 to 6 months old. It was filled to capacity. Aisles were narrow, and it was musty and hot, but by the time everyone had arrived, we were more than ready to climb into the bunk beds provided.

We alighted the next morning into ankle-deep water, but luckily permission had been given to vacate the shelter. Other than lots and lots of rain, we had only been visited by the fringes of Flora. Captain Kendig collected his soggy family, who was delighted to return to high ground, a shower, and clean, dry clothing.

The second evacuation for this capricious lady was the next afternoon. It had been determined that the underground shelters were untenable because of the flooding, and others in them elsewhere were to be sheltered instead in the highschool gymnasium. Not so those of us in the underground hospital, since the emergency equipment was already in place, with no time to relocate it. So, back we came for another soggy day.

Hospital Corpsman, Bob Cohoon, kept our bunker as acceptable as possible with his constant bailing and mopping, and this time, my children and I had brought footwear that could stand up to the water. It was a challenge to keep them occupied with activities on the bed rather than wading up and down the narrow aisles.

During our confinement, we were issued K-rations at mealtime. K-rations are designed for troops in combat, high in carbohydrates and rich in nutrients, all of which are ideal for troops tromping through fields all day never knowing when they might get their next meal. But, for people cooped up in a small shelter with no physical activity, they produced a monstrous assault on our digestive systems. Mine did not recover for weeks!

It was a great relief when, by the next morning, the all-clear sounded, and we were once again released to our own quarters. Bob was at the door, hat in hand, hoping we had enjoyed his hospitality and would return soon . . . little dreaming we would do just that. The very next morning, we were back again, awakened by the Base alarm siren.

Bob's purpose in Building One of the underground hospital was, as he put it,
"To get the doctor when your groans get five minutes apart."
Luckily no such emergency arose. And during our third descent to the damp sanctuary, Bob performed heroically. As he wielded his ever-present mop, he would frequently rend the underground atmosphere with, "Oh what a beautiful morning . . . oh what a beautiful day . . . who would want a more beautiful way . . . ay . . . to spend the day in Guantanamo Bay." No one had ordered Bob to keep his sense of humor long after everyone else had lost theirs.

Fifty hours in a hurricane shelter were yet another of those bizarre incidents that seemed to plague our entire experience in Gitmo. No hurricane had hit Cuba in the previous 19 years, yet during our short tour, Hurricane Flora had not only threatened the Base, veered away, turned and come back before leaving a second time, but had reversed her path for one final assault before disappearing out to sea. In spite of the inconvenience, the damage to the Base was minor, with no loss of life. Others were not so fortunate. In the interior of Cuba, Hurricane Flora had killed at least 1200 people.

Later that month, on the first anniversary of the Cuban Missile Crisis, the following article appeared on the front page of the Gitmo Review:

October 22, 1963 **Reminiscence of a Crisis** by Pat Kendig

The first anniversary of the Cuban Crisis is being greeted with mixed emotions. As significant as the evacuation was to those of us who experienced it, ours was only one very small part of the Crisis. "Newsweek" magazine, in an eight-page summary, allowed us one sentence: "The dependents of the United States Naval Base at Guantanamo Bay, Cuba, were evacuated."

As October 22nd approaches, there is little here at Gitmo to physically remind us of the event. The concentrated defensive positions below Chapel Hill have become commonplace. We allow ourselves only a brief moment of reflection when the *Upshur Club* badge turns up among the toys. The gripes about Gitmo that had so completely disappeared upon our return last December, have recurred again in full voice.

Statistically, a total of 2811 dependents were evacuated from our Base by 5 p.m. on October 22, 1962. Five Marine Corps troop transport planes carried 379 of them, including 23 patients. The Portsmouth Naval Hospital received those patients as they required continued hospitalization. The youngest of those evacuated was four days old. One expectant mother was dropped off at Cherry point Hospital and delivered a seven-pound girl. The remainder of the "evacuees" arrived in Norfolk by ship. The seaplane tender, Duxbury Bay carried 351; the refrigeration ship Hyades held 286, and the tank landing ship Desoto County carried 92. The remaining1703 sailed aboard the USNS Upshur.

At home on Gitmo, we left 307 officers and 3000 men of the Navy and Marine Corps. As reinforcements for them, waves of Boeing C-130 jet transports began arriving before dawn on October 21st. Each plane carried 125 fully equipped Marines. Within 5 ½ hours, this airlift was completed. Others arrived within 36 hours aboard ships until some 45,000 Marines stood ready to invade Cuba, with 100,000 more Marines ready to back them up. Marine Corps Commandant General David M. Shoup, is quoted as saying after he inspected the defenses: "I think I'd rather be on this side of the fence than that side."

It's not my place, nor am I qualified to pass judgment on the evacuation. I witnessed many individual cases of personal sacrifice, brotherly love, compassion, and charity. Perhaps we needed the evacuation to help us see things in their proper perspective again.

I find it very significant that last October, with her 30 strategically placed medium-range missiles, Russia was threatening to blow the United States off the face of the earth, and this October, she is entreating us to sell her about $170 millions worth of wheat to feed those living in her "thriving economy". Who knows what next year may bring. Perhaps with prayer, a real peace, with no walls and no gates anywhere!

THE *Gitmo Review*

A WEEKLY PUBLICATION U.S. Naval Base, Guantanamo Bay, Cuba October 12, 1963

GITMO REMEMBERS FLORA

22-1   Prior to Flora, a hurricane had not hit Cuba in 19 years

23

Backdoor Diplomacy

Life continued in the rest of the world, but I felt detached from most of it. A simple headline in the Gitmo Gazette would alert us to national and international events, but their impact was lost on me.

On Monday, June 3, 1963, the headline announced that Pope John XXIII had died slowly, in prayer and suffering, in the fifth year of his reign:
His stout peasant's heart carried him through more than three days of final agony that was relieved only by lapses into comas. [i]

Then, on Friday, August 9, 1963, difficulty breathing resulted in the death of Patrick Bouvier Kennedy, the infant son of President John F. Kennedy and his wife, Jackie. His birth was five and one-half weeks premature and he weighed less than 5 pounds.

On November 22, 1963, I was sitting on my patio reading while the children played in the back yard. My neighbor to the right, Betsy Neal, came over and said, "President Kennedy has just been shot." Again, since our only source of news was the Gitmo Gazette, a mimeographed sheet circulated daily to all base quarters, I found it hard to comprehend what she was telling me. Someone had just relayed this information to her husband, Captain Robert Neal, over ham radio. We had no details, nor did we know how serious it might be. Within hours, we learned the shot had been fatal.

Due to our separation from a consistent news source, the realization that the 35th President of the United

States had been shot and killed just didn't sink in. I went about my activities much as I had every day, trying to absorb it into consciousness. How could this have happened in broad daylight? What would the transfer of power to Vice President Lyndon Johnson mean to the Nation? And most importantly, where did he stand on issues critical to our daily lives in this military outpost?

The following editorial, appeared in the Gitmo Gazette:
The sun set upon Guantanamo Bay and the world had a new martyr. But not even the setting of the sun came as it usually does on this most tragic and singular day – November 22, 1963. The moon was high in the black sky and a solitary star shone over the horizon. And yet, the atmosphere glowed dull red to the East, where 30 minutes before the sun had set.

The President of the United States of America, John F. Kennedy, was dead at the hand of an assassin. A stunned and subdued world waited, watched, and prayed. As many tried to grasp the magnitude of the event, some of us recalled that another American President, Abraham Lincoln, had been murdered by a killer's bullet 99 years ago.

The man who succeeded Lincoln was President Andrew Johnson, Then as now, the United States was in a struggle that affected every citizen, and much of the world. Then, as now, Americans reacted with shock, anguish, grief and sadness…and courage and resolve. [2]

*

I followed some of the news about the President's death on our one TV channel, but the life of a mother with two active children is not conducive to sitting for long periods of time in front of a television set, so I switched to the radio, and continued to go about my daily chores. I was sweeping the kitchen floor when the announcer said the casket of my Commander in Chief was being brought into the Rotunda of the

Capital. The voice receded and the strains of "Hail to the Chief" filled my kitchen. The swirls of dust caused by my sweeping swam out of focus, and I was forced to lean on the broom while I sobbed.

Soon after our return to Cuba after the evacuation, I received an official form from the Department of Defense asking me to itemize the expenses I had incurred because of the evacuation. If I had receipts for these, a check in reimbursement would be sent to me. I was able to find some relevant receipts and sent my request along accordingly.

Early in December of 1963, my reimbursement check arrived. Since this was money I had never expected to receive, and because of its arrival shortly before Christmas, I regarded it as a gift. I used it to buy a 15-piece hand-painted Hummel nativity set I had seen and admired at the PX. Every Christmas thereafter, when friends would admire our elegant nativity scene, I would proudly proclaim that it was a gift from President Kennedy.

One hot afternoon in late 1963, I heard a gentle knock at the back door. I had to listen carefully to see if it was actually a knock or my imagination. When I heard it again, I headed through the house, and was surprised to see two Cuban men on my doorstep. We often saw Cuban women (who served as domestic workers) strolling around the neighborhood, visiting with each other, but the only indigenous men we ever encountered were Mr. Henry, the gardener from Barbados, and his only employee, Chang.

The shorter and darker of these two men at my door stepped forward and introduced himself as Carlos. He then presented Roberto, and went on to tell me in broken English that Roberto was the brother of Mierna

Suarez, the Cuban exile who had been our 'guest' when we first arrived in Cuba. Roberto, thus properly introduced, presented me with a large box of chocolates.

Mierna had told me she had a brother who looked somewhat like me, with light brown hair, fair skin, and freckles. The man named Roberto certainly resembled this description.

I was eager to hear news of Mierna. It was a very hot time of the day, so I invited the two men in under the cool of the fan and had them take a seat. When I offered something to drink, they waved it away, but I insisted and poured ice tea, into which they dumped the copious spoons of sugar that was the local habit.

Conversation was laborious, but I wanted to learn what had happened to Mierna. Eventually I was able to understand she had landed safely in Miami, and had been there for several months before learning that her husband had, indeed, lost his life during the Bay of Pigs invasion in April of 1961.

Because Roberto had been associated with the Cuban military who opposed the Fidelistas, he had sought exile on the base, and was working as a refrigerator repairman. He had fled for his life and left behind a wife and twin daughters. He showed me their pictures and talked of them with deep affection. It was difficult for me to imagine how he expected to be reunited with them.

When Billy and Colleen awakened from their naps, the two men were in their element. The children brought out some of their toys, and the men were soon engrossed in watching and participating with them in their play.

From then on, in the first week of every month I could expect a gentle knock at the back door. I came to learn this was the week in which Cuban exiles were paid. The second time Roberto gifted me with yet another box of chocolates, I had Carlos tell him this was not necessary. But I underestimated Roberto's resolve to somehow repay me for giving his sister sanctuary. On succeeding visits he brought toys for the children.

Over the months, Roberto told me Mierna had married in Miami and moved to New Jersey with her new husband. Before we left the Base, I learned she had given birth to a strapping son (9 pounds some ounces) and that both she and the baby were doing well. I had always hoped for some word from Mierna, but because she could not write English, I didn't really expect it would happen. I was thrilled to learn that not only had she survived her abrupt transplantation, but had been able to build a new life for herself in a foreign country.

Another frequent backdoor visitor was Julio. As Supply Officer of the Marine Barracks, one of my husband's responsibilities was operation of the Base laundry, which had been run by the Wu family for as long as anyone could remember. Julio was Mr. Wu's son.

Like Bob Work, Mr. Wu had been brought from the U.S. as an employee of Public Works. In due time, he had met and married a Cuban woman. Their son, Julio, was an interesting combination of genes. He had Asian features, but at 16, had become a tall and lanky throwback from one of his Cuban ancestors.

My husband had decided to send our sheets to the laundry as a way of monitoring the quality of their work, as well as a means of saving wear and tear on our washer/dryer. If either of these appliances failed, there was no running down to the local Sears to buy a new one. It might be months before one could be shipped, and repair was minimal to nonexistent. Therefore, on Tuesday of each week, Julio would arrive at our back door and leave a neatly wrapped package in brown paper containing our clean bed linen. He would exchange this for our three sets of soiled sheets which I had left at the back door, prepared into a bundle by tying the four corners of one of the double sheets together.

Before too many months, I noticed some of our pillowcases were badly pulled at the seams. Pillowcases are normally not a wear item, and I didn't think too much more about it until one day I observed Julio in the process of the laundry pick-up. The first thing he did was untie my neat bundle, and then begin to stuff the entire load, one sheet and pillow case at a time, into one of the pillow cases.

As he was doing this, I rushed to the bedroom to get the damaged pillowcase. Hurrying to the back door, I showed Julio the pulled seams and demonstrated how stuffing all the bed linen into one pillowcase was the cause. He smiled agreeably, but when I had gone into the house, I glanced back through the open wooden louvers to see him continuing where he had left off before I interrupted him.

Over the months, my neighbors and I had been unable to figure out exactly what language Julio spoke. He greeted all our attempts at conversation with a big grin, but we never knew whether this signified comprehension or not. By turns, I had tried both English and the little Spanish I had learned from Herberto. On this occasion, I assumed Julio had not deliberately ignored me. It was just some kind of communication problem.

Armed with resolve, I came out the back door again, damaged pillowcase in hand. With renewed vigor, I shook my head and waggled my finger at what he was doing. I proceeded to take the sheets out of the pillowcase and prepare them in their original four-cornered bundle. Julio looked at me like any teenager would look at a deranged adult, picked up the bundle, and headed for his laundry truck. The damage to the pillowcases continued, and I had to assume that whatever language Julio knew was not one we shared.

On the first anniversary of our return to Gitmo, the following was published:

December 22, 1963 **Scene Around Gitmo** by Pat Kendig
A Day to Remember

Twas three days before Christmas, and all through our home
Memories, like echoes, had started to roam
Of a time in December when it just wasn't clear
If or where we'd have Christmas at all last year.
Enroute on a ship was all Santa's loot
Including the tree trim and our car to boot
When out of the blue came the ring of a bell
Western Union had a wonderful message to tell
"You and your children, if any, proceed
On 19 December, with all you might need
To Brooklyn for passage aboard a fine ship
To take you to Gitmo, so have a good trip.

As I drew in my head and was turning around
Down from heaven this miracle had come with a bound
Who cares if we didn't have trimmings or toys
Daddy would be all our needs … all our joys.

Utah was fogged in, so we took a train
Overnight to Denver, then boarded a plane.
And finally, in Brooklyn, we got on the ship
And eternities later, we finished our trip.

151

"Twas three days before Christmas we landed ashore
On a day I'll remember forever more!
There were many big signs, but the largest in size
Was in red and gold and said, "Welcome Marine Wives!"

We clung to our Daddy, and said a quick prayer
If this is a dream, it just isn't fair!
Unlike our departure, now everyone cried
With pent-up emotions kept two months inside.

And there in our home, wrapped with splendor galore
Was the tree and the toys, returned two days before.
So after last Christmas, one thought makes me pause;
Don't try to tell me there is no Santa Claus!

*

Christmas Day on Guantanamo was a surreal experience. It was not reminiscent of any Christmas Day in **my** memory. The sun was shining brightly, and it was 82 degrees. After Mass and all the presents had been opened, Colleen and Billy, not yet saddled with tradition, were asking when we were going to the pool. About this time, there came a knock at the back door.

My husband opened the door, and there was Julio, and it wasn't even Tuesday. Instead of the usual bundle of clean laundry, he held a large circular silver-plated tray on which was a tea pot and matching sugar and creamer. This he handed to my husband. He then extracted from his pocket an envelope addressed carefully to "Captain Kendig".

Bill placed the silver service on the entry table and took the envelope, as I watched with curiosity. After he had opened it, I edged close enough to see a brief hand-scrawled Christmas greeting signed by Mr. Wu.

152

Expressing his appreciation for the gesture, my husband gently handed back the silver tray and its contents, explaining to Julio that it was against Military rules for him to accept a gift from an employee under his jurisdiction.

It took Julio awhile to understand my husband was refusing the gift, but eventually, gift in hand, he shuffled back down the driveway. I watched him leave nearly in tears with disappointment. It was a handsome silver coffee service, with graceful footed legs and scalloped tray.

We were on our way out the door a bit later, heading for relief at the pool, when we nearly collided with Julio. He had the silver tray and its contents in his arms. Without any preamble, and with no accompanying card, he practically thrust the silver service at my husband and said,
"For Mrs. Kendig!"

[1] Gitmo Gazette – U.S. Naval Base, Guantanamo Bay, Cuba -June 3, 1963.
[2] Pitchford, Douglas – Gitmo Gazette – U.S. Naval Base, Guantanamo Bay, Cuba – November 22, 1963.

Phone 9247   Date FRI., NOV. 22, 1963   WGBY Radio (1340) TV (Ch. 8)

PRESIDENT KENNEDY DEAD

DALLAS, TEXAS NOV. 22 (AP) -- President John F. Kennedy, thirty-sixth President of the United States, was shot to death today by a hidden assassin armed with a high-powered rifle.

Kennedy, 46, lived about an hour after a sniper cut him down as his limousine left downtown Dallas.

Phone 9247   Date Monday, June 3, 1963   WGBY Radio (1340) TV (Ch. 8)

POPE JOHN XXIII DEAD!

DEATH COMES SLOWLY AT 1:49 P.M

VATICAN CITY, June 3 (UPI) - Pope John XXIII, one of the greatest popes in the history of the Roman Catholic Church,

23-1   National and international events seemed far removed from the Gitmo scene

SCENE AROUND GITMO

A DAY TO REMEMBER

'Twas three days before Christmas, and all through our
    home
Memories, like echoes, had started to roam
Of a time in December when it just wasn't clear
If or where we'd have Christmas at all last year.

Enroute on a ship was all Santa's loot
Including the tree trim and our car to boot
When out of the blue came the ring of a bell
Western Union had a wonderful message to tell
"You and your children, if any, proceed
On 19 December, with all you might need
To Brooklyn for passage aboard a fine ship
To take you to Gitmo, so have a good trip."

As I drew in my head and was turning around
Down from heaven this miracle had come with a bound
Who cares if we didn't have trimmings or toys
Daddy would be all our needs — all our joys.

Utah was fogged in, so we took a train
Overnight to Denver, then boarded a plane.
And finally, in Brooklyn, we got on the ship
And eternities later, we finished our trip.

'Twas three days before Christmas we landed ashore
On a day I'll remember forever more!
There were many big signs, but the largest in size
Was in red and gold and said "Welcome Marine Wives!"
We clung to our Daddy and said a quick prayer
If this is a dream, it just isn't fair!
Unlike our departure, now everyone cried
With pent-up emotions kept two months inside.

And there in our home, wrapped with splendor galore
Was the tree and the toys, returned two days before.
So after last Christmas, one thought makes me pause —
Don't ever tell me there is no Santa Claus!

                                    Pat Kendig

23-2   Author's poem as published in Gitmo Review

24

And Not a Drop to Drink

In the year following our return to Gitmo, there was a run on the maternity ward of the Naval Hospital. The record was six births in one week when there were normally only two in a month. When I added to these statistics, I was greeted by Corpsman Bob Cohoon, our underground hurricane shelter host. I almost didn't recognize him without his mop.

On Tuesday, January 28, 1964, the following notice appeared on the front page of the Gitmo Gazette:

Scene Around Gitmo

Gitmo Review columnist, Pat Kendig, produced a 6 pound, 15 ounce news item by the name of John James Kendig at the Naval Hospital here yesterday, January 27. Father of the new arrival is Captain William F. Kendig, USMC, of Marine Barracks. The staffs of the Gitmo Gazette and Review extend special congratulations on the arrival of young Mr. Kendig to our favorite stringer. [1]

And, on February 6, 1964, the day Johnny was to be baptized into the Roman Catholic Church, Castro cut off the outside water supply to the Base. Since I had completed the super-human task of getting Johnny and his siblings dressed and ready for departure just as the word came around about this newest crisis, I declared this child was going to be baptized, water or no water. I knew, of course, that Holy Water was always on hand, but it seemed too much of a coincidence not to make some comment.

Our Proxy Godfather, Lt. Cdr. F.X (Gus) Brady arrived out of breath because he had been in the Admiral's office helping to deal with this latest crisis. Father William F. Fallon had holy water in reserve and the main attraction slept through the whole thing.

President Lyndon B. Johnson and his advisers met to decide whether retaliatory measures should be taken against Fidel Castro because of his most recent harassment. The Cuban leader was seeking to use this water-deprivation as a means for obtaining the release of 36 Cuban fishermen held by Florida authorities. President Johnson reported there was no doubt the Cuban fishermen arrested off the Florida coast were inside the territorial waters of the United States. The Cuban government insisted the fishermen had been seized in international waters. Castro further claimed he had no desire to harm civilians, including women and children at the base, and as proof of this, he would supply water for their needs for one hour a day, from 8 to 9 in the morning.

According to clippings from the Salt Lake Tribune sent by my mother, Castro's cutting off the water supply to Guantanamo was more of than 'inconvenience' than a danger to military operations. The Base had approximately five days supply at the normal usage rate. Advance measures had been taken months earlier to make certain enough water to last 12 days would be in storage at Guantanamo, and in anticipation of Castro's action, the United States was prepared to move water to the Base indefinitely by ship from Port Everglades, Florida. The article went on to report:

A high official also said there were no plans to evacuate the 2,400 women and children from the 31-square mile American naval base niched in the southeast corner of Communist Cuba. An emergency air and sea lift took the dependents off the island when war was threatened there in October 1962. [2]

I was especially glad when I saw this in print! In a companion article, the Salt Lake Tribune reported:

During the 1962 missile crisis, Castro insisted that the United States withdraw from Guantanamo. The United States response to this demand was to send thousands of Marine reinforcements to the base. Castro did not change his tune, but he lost his battle . . . As long as communism rules Cuba, the United States can expect harassment against the Guantanamo Base. But Castro also can expect his actions to fail. The United States is not about to withdraw from its important naval fortification in the Caribbean. [3]

Then, Rear Admiral J. D. Bulkeley effectively cut Castro's water off. Our base newsletter reported:

At 6:15 p.m. on Monday, February 17 (and mark that date, as it may well become a very famous one in the annals of the free world's struggle against tyranny), fourteen U.S. newsmen joined a group of Base officials and a working party at a site just inside the Northeast Gate for a public pipe-cutting ceremony which was Admiral Bulkeley's answer to Castro's trumped-up charges that the Base had been 'stealing' water from the Yateras pumping plant. While cameras and tape-recorders ground away, workmen cut a 38-inch, 300 pound section from the 14-inch pipeline which had carried water to this Base for more than 20 years, and then completely sealed off the pipeline.

RADM Bulkeley ordered this action taken to prove to the Free World that the Navy is not using any of Castro's water, and does not intend to in the future. [4]

The absolutely dry conditions in and around the pipe were indisputable evidence that NO water had flowed through this pipe for a long time, contrary to Castro's claim that he had been pumping 110 thousand gallons daily for use of the women and children on the Base.

In a companion article, the Admiral was given a special bottle of water from the *USS Abatan*, docked off shore. We called it "the water ship", and it carried a reverse osmosis water distilling plant from which potable water would be made available to the Base.

Excerpts to a letter I wrote to my family in Salt Lake about all this follows:

February 7, 1964

Dear Mom, Dad, and Jack,

The official scoop from DC at this time is that without water rationing, our Base has enough in storage to last 12 days. With rationing (which began at 6:00 p.m. February 6) we have enough to last 25 days.

Johnny was baptized February 6 at 4:45 p.m   It was a beautiful Baptism! I had fed him at 3:30, and he slept through the whole thing. Made a face when he tasted the salt and opened his eyes when Father very carefully poured the water over his head. He wore the same dress Colleen and Billy had worn for their Baptisms and looked precious with his little round head and dark hair.   Love you all, Pat

*

Shortly thereafter, we received **Naval Base Instruction 11330.2D – Subject: Fresh Water; Control of**. There followed specific instructions for Water Conditions. A new banner on the front page of The Gitmo Gazette, opposite the weather, would indicate either water condition Charlie, Bravo, or Alpha, depending on the situation. Then, in a special column at the bottom left-hand edge would be:

Today's Water Report . . . An example follows:
Water on hand at 8 a.m., 13,568,000 gallons. Yesterday the Base used 1,240,000 gallons. The tanker Suamico is en route to Port Everglades to load 1.4 million gallons. The tanker Tullulah is now in the Florida port loading.

It was something of a challenge to care for a newborn between February 6th and 17th with three water periods a day, but it certainly beat the alternative . . . evacuation! I'd been there, done that!

---

[1] Gitmo Gazette, Tuesday, January 28, 1964.
[2] Salt Lake Tribune, February 7, 1964
[3] Ibid
[4] Gitmo Gazette, Wednesday, February 19, 1964

24-1 Author and infant son, John, on Baptism day

25

Where the Buffalo Roamed

In February 1964, the lead article in the Gitmo Gazette reported the following Defense Department announcement:

No more families of military and civilian personnel will be sent to Guantanamo Naval Base in Cuba, and dependents now there will be removed over the next two years.
Assistant Secretary of Defense Arthur Sylvester announced this action as a further step in the process of making the Guantanamo Naval Base entirely self-sufficient, and to improve the garrison posture of the forces there. Dependents now on station will be returned to the U.S. at the normal expiration of their sponsors' regular tour of duty. [1]

The article went on to say that the 3,000 dependents currently on the Base had been subjected to new Cuban pressure in the form of a cut-off of fresh water. It also reported that future unaccompanied military tours on Gitmo would be shortened to a year in order to minimize the time of family separations.

The first veteran of the evacuation, Karen Morris and her family, left shortly thereafter. She was the one who had the horrible experience on the Duxbury Bay when she and her children were all seasick the first night aboard. The next month we lost my dear friend and mentor, Claire Seibert and her family. It had been a privilege to live next door to this loving and considerate woman. Simply by her manner, her courtesy, and her integrity, Claire was a role model for how to live a life well.

As the months passed and more and more of those who had become 'family' departed, I wrote the following article.

March 14, 1964 **Scene Around Gitmo** by Pat Kendig

I have been feeling strangely like the American buffalo lately . . . soon to become extinct. I find myself staring off into space, especially the space occupied by the lovely Guantanamo Bay.

As a romanticist, I think mostly about the intangibles of our community. The wives forbidden to come here will never smell the special odor of a bloom of Ah Susannah. They will never hear the soft call of the Cuban dove while watching the sunrise silhouette the ships in the Bay.

Most of all, my thoughts concern that long year those wives will be unable to share with their husbands. No letter can convey what actually happens during a defensive exercise. The husband will receive letters about familiar surroundings, but it will be impossible for his wife to achieve a real picture of the Gitmo scene through mere words on paper or a photo, and she will have lost one complete year of shared experience.

In my estimation, there has been no event in the last 18 months that could be called a 'hardship'. The Gitmo adventure has been more than worth four evacuations (three for hurricane Flora). It's been worth caring for a ten-day-old infant with limited water. It's been worth those phone calls in the middle of the night and those interrupted meals with no explanation. The foregoing are trivial, because to me there is only one real hardship, and that is separation from my husband.

*

Base Commander, Admiral Bulkeley, responded to all of this in his typical feisty fashion. On March 24, 1964, his statement was published in the Gitmo Gazette:

I am appalled that the actions of Fidel Castro in the recent water incident have made changes necessary in our way of life in Gitmo. Let me reiterate at this time that there is no cause for alarm...and that there are NO PLANS FOR EVACUATION other than by transfer at the end of a normal tour of duty. . . . Our only real problem right now is one that requires the complete cooperation of all hands . . . and stringent water conservation practices to keep our daily consumption below one-million gallons until such time as our new salt water conversion plant is in operation.

The next problem is to train the fleet better than ever and show the stateside citizens that there is not one cry-baby in the Naval service here in Gitmo . . . civilian or military. You have certainly cooperated with me and I heartily appreciate it. Let's discharge our duties to the United States with courage, verve, and élan! [2]

In early Spring of 1964, Marines guarding the Gitmo gate and fence line were subjected to harassment in the form of rock throwing and shouted insults. In addition, Cubans put up floodlights outside the northeast gate that focused strong beams on the guard post, which almost blinded the sentries.

Medal of Honor Winner Bulkeley, decided on a counter measure. He instructed his people to pick a site on a hill 75 yards inside the gate where they laid out a circular concrete slab 30 feet in diameter and six inches thick. After the concrete hardened, they painted the anchor-globe-and-eagle Marine Corps emblem in full red, gold, and white. A spokesman for the Marine Corps said it was probably the biggest Marine emblem in the world. The Cubans outside the gate found that when they turned on their floodlights at night, they couldn't aim them at the Marine sentries without illuminating the defiant Marine emblem. Soon thereafter, the Admiral reported there were no more floodlights.

I tried to do my part to keep up morale, but all of my newspaper columns, no matter how well-intentioned, seemed tinged with a melancholy overtone. Excerpts from some of these follow.

March 14, 1964 **Scene Around Gitmo** by Pat Kendig

. . . Let's contemplate those sounds that belong exclusively to Gitmo . . . The most familiar and reassuring are the Public Works Center whistles at morning, noon, and evening. I say 'reassuring' because unconsciously we all listen for them and possibly set the pattern of our day by them. . . . Most uniquely a part of the Gitmo scene are the sirens that announce the beginning of another Defensive Exercise.

Since most of the Points on Base are peninsular, the ship's bells and their loudspeaker systems carry across the water to our residences. And even though it might just be a practice, how I love to hear the band music transmitted across the Points by the water and breezes. My favorite Gitmo sound occurs at 10 o'clock (or 2200 in military gargon) when the eerie and forlorn strains of "Taps" float across from Marine Site 2. I know I shall never again hear Taps without being reminded of our unique Gitmo adventure.

June 13, 1964 **Scene Around Gitmo** by Pat Kendig

I recognize that car . . . so I wave . . . and sometimes honk as it passes me. Rarely do I need to check to see who's driving the car. . . .And, how distracting are the feelings when that familiar car approaches during these 'end times'. You know darn well you put that particular neighbor on the boat or plane last month, and you even remember they sold their car before leaving. But this head knowledge is not enough to stop the emotional reaction you experience each time you see that car. A sudden and uncontrollable emptiness embraces you as you experience all over again how much you still miss the former owners.

July 4, 1964 **Scene Around Gitmo** by Pat Kendig

You will never again celebrate the Fourth of July quite like you are celebrating today here in Gitmo. At the parade, there is no pushing, shoving, unfriendly crowd. And it isn't necessary to drive for miles looking for a place to park.
Maybe the sun was just as hot where you spent the Fourth as a kid, but when you got thirsty, did someone put a free bottle of pop in your hand? And were the balloons and ice cream also free of charge?

. . .We misplaced our youngsters a couple of times last year. In a city, I would have immediately panicked. All we did during Gitmo's celebration was circulate through the sea of familiar faces, making spot inquiries. A neighbor soon told us where they were.

All around us, the people of our 'small town' are oozing away like quick-sand as 'operation phase-out' continues. We know we are living in a dying community. We feel it more each time we go to the commissary and the parking lot is emptier. We feel it poignantly at church, where the attendance diminishes appreciably each week. Sure we're a dying community, but if the exuberance of those remaining has anything to do with it, we're not dead yet. So today, let's have a bang-up Fourth of July. Let's die on a crescendo!

---

[1] Gitmo Gazette – U. S. Naval Base, Guantanamo Bay, Cuba – February 12, 1964.
[2] Ibid – February 13, 1964

25-1   Neighbors, Lt. Colonel Kenneth D. and Claire Seibert, in front of Ken's jeep

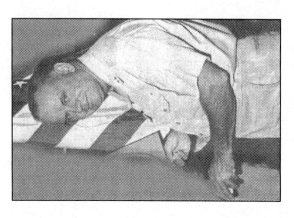

UNITED STATES NAVAL BASE
NAVY 116, BOX 14
CARE OF FLEET POST OFFICE
NEW YORK, N. Y. 09593

In Reply Refer to:
NB37:001:MLl:wd
1650
30 November 1964

From: Commander, U. S. Naval Base, Guantanamo Bay, Cuba
To: Pat Kendig
       1693 Battery Creek Road
       Beaufort, South Carolina

Subj: Letter of Appreciation

1. During the recent tour of duty in Guantanamo Bay of your
husband, Captain William F. Kendig, USMC, you performed an
outstanding community service to the residents of the Naval Base
through your regular contribution of a newspaper column for the
GITMO REVIEW entitled, "Scene Around Gitmo".

2. We of the Navy and Marine Corps are indeed fortunate to
have the volunteer services of people such as yourself who are
willing to give freely of their own time and talent so that others
may benefit.

3. On behalf of the military and civilian personnel and their
dependents I wish to convey our appreciation to you for a job
"Well Done". Our best wishes go with you and yours in all
future endeavors. Your presence here in Guantanamo Bay
will be missed.

JOHN D. BULKELEY
Rear Admiral, U. S. Navy

25-2   Letter of Appreciation to author for
       her columns in the Gitmo Review
       from Admiral John D. Bulkeley,
       Commander of the Guantanamo Bay
       Naval Base

Epilogue

In keeping with the ironies of our two-year Odyssey, it only seems appropriate that on a sunny afternoon in August of 1964, we left our Gitmo paradise on the USNS *Upshur*, the same vessel on which we had been evacuated. As I stood on that deck watching the island of Cuba recede, I recalled how I had felt standing on that same deck as we docked in Norfolk on October 25, 1962. The quest for home that had motivated me then returned with a vengeance.

What would await us at my husband's new assignment in Parris Island, South Carolina? What kind of a community would my children encounter? In spite of the political uncertainties of Gitmo life, our children had felt secure and cherished as part of a larger community. They had enjoyed a life with no restraints and no concerns about things like traffic or strangers. Whatever awaited us would be a sea change for them.

The children were not the only ones who were to find reentry difficult. We arrived in New York as Hurricane Dora was heading toward the coast of South Carolina. We had no choice but to try to beat her. We arrived to find the Parris Island Marine Recruit Depot closed for Hurricane Condition Two. An accommodating Marine Officer secured us one room with two beds in the Officer's Guest House, and opened his Mess Hall to provide us scrambled eggs for dinner. A meal had never tasted so good!

Fervent though it might have been, the quest to create a home for our children remained elusive. No base housing was available, so we made a down payment on a small residence in the city of Beaufort. After moving in and beginning renovations, we learned we could not qualify for the loan because we had never owed money. It had never been necessary, as we had never lived anywhere in our entire marriage except on a Marine Base.

Our next move was to a small rental unit on a very busy street where we survived until Base housing was available. Excerpts from the letter I wrote to enclose with our Christmas cards follows:

December 1964

We have not dropped off the face of the earth . . . only been "phased out", but therein lies another tale.

The highlight of our year was the birth of our son, John James. He arrived on January 27th, weighing one ounce less than seven pounds. Ten days later, the very hour of Johnny's Baptism, Castro turned off the water supplying Guantanamo Naval Base.

The Water Crisis was hectic, especially with a new baby. We saved wash water for mopping and mop water for flushing commodes. Shortly thereafter, Washington ruled there would be a gradual "phase-out" of dependents. We who were already there could stay until our sponsor's tour of duty terminated. Bill's replacement could not bring his family.

I had long had my name on the waiting list for a flight to Port au Prince, Haiti. Just as my name reached the top, these trips were stopped because of an invasion by the Dominican Republic on Papa Doc's territory. In August, one week before our departure from Gitmo, they resumed the trips. I was so elated to be going that I didn't stop to think of the risk involved until we boarded and there were only 14 people on a 48-passenger plane. There was no incident and we had a delightfully different day amid drum and maraca music, voodoo carvings, mahogany ware, beautiful fluid art work, and the all-pervading presence of Duvalier, with a life-size signboard likeness every block, lest you forget.

Our departure from Gitmo and final arrival at Bill's new duty station (Parris Island, South Carolina) were fraught with adversity. We were due to sail on Monday, August 24th, but Hurricane Cleo blew up that schedule and we didn't sail until the following Wednesday. We arrived in New York harbor at night and all of the ships lights were added to those of the New York skyline. It was quite a "welcome home".

The congestion, smell, and noise of New York made us immediately homesick for our small, familiar Gitmo. In spite of the trials of getting settled, we are very fond of the quaint town of Beaufort, one of the Nation's oldest.

Thinking back over the year, it had seemed a full one, but actually seeing it written down, I am suddenly very tired! I'll be quite content to let someone else make history next year.

*

I breathed a huge sigh of relief when we finally secured Base housing in August of the following year. It was only a short walk to the Officer's Club and pool, as well as to the grade school where Colleen would begin kindergarten.

One afternoon, shortly after our move to the base, I was on a step stool hanging curtains in our dining room when my husband came in the back door saying he needed to talk to me. I asked if he could wait until I'd finished hanging the curtain. He said, "I don't think you're going to want to finish hanging that curtain." He had received orders for Viet Nam.

It hit me like a dash of cold water to be on the move again before I'd even had the chance to finish unpacking or enjoying the conveniences of this new home. I was again faced with the decision about whether to stay in the vicinity of the Marine Base for convenience of all the accoutrements (PX, commissary, medical care), or settle elsewhere for my husband's 13-month tour of duty where I would not be reminded of my solitude every time I saw the Marine uniform? In another one of those insights, my heart knew that the only place for a woman on her own with three children under five years of age was with family, and so I again made the decision to return to my archetypical home.

Between the time my husband told me about his orders for Viet Nam and our relocation to Salt Lake, we learned he had been passed over for the second time for the rank of Major, which means an automatic, but honorable, separation from the Marine Corps. I have always had the feeling he had volunteered for the Viet Nam duty, hoping it would enhance his chances for promotion. I vacillated during the 13 months he was gone between denial and abject terror concerning our chances of survival as civilians.

When Bill returned from Viet Nam, we rented a home in Vista, California for his final obligatory tour of duty at Camp Pendleton, California. During the unsettled time waiting for the end of our Marine Corps career, the memories of home that had been established in Salt Lake acted as a magnet for me. Luckily, when I asked Bill where he thought we should settle after his separation, his first choice was Salt Lake. We returned there in 1968, which was providential, because my mother died in 1969, and I'd have never believed it unless I'd been there. She had always taken care of the rest of us. How could she have been sick, much less dead?

The pattern of an absentee father and husband that had been established during our Marine Corps career continued into civilian life. Bill accepted a job with a defense contractor that required frequent business travel. And not too long thereafter, he who had always felt that my working would be a negative reflection on his ability to support his family, said, "Looks like you're going to have to get a job." I did just that working at entry-level 'jobs' that required no overtime or travel, so that at least one parent could maintain a home for our children.

After my mother's death, my father devoted himself to our three children. I would drop them off with him on my way to work. He would deliver them to school in the winter and to day camp in the summer. He was also the one who took them to the doctor/dentist or stayed home with anyone sick. One day as we were driving to his home, Billy said, "I guess we have just about the best Grandpa in the whole world!" This gentle man died in 1974.

By 1985, I was alone in the empty nest. Our oldest son, Bill, was the first to marry. He and his wife left Salt Lake for Baton Rouge, Louisiana, where he graduated from the Louisiana State University Law School. They and my two granddaughters make their home in Shreveport, Louisiana, where Bill is a partner in the law firm of Rice and Kendig.

Colleen graduated from the University of Utah Nursing School, and married a Salt Lake man. They are currently living in Ouray, Colorado with their son and daughter. She is Clinical Coordinator and Case Manager of the Hospice of the Uncompahgre Valley. I once asked her how she is able to deal with the terminally ill on a routine basis, and she said, "I just look on every patient as if they are Grandpa, and care for them as I yearned to care for Grandpa if only I had been old enough and skilled enough when he was dying".

John accepted a job in New York right out of high school, returned a year later to pursue the Fine Arts Program at the University of Utah for two years, married and moved to Seattle. He endeavors to establish himself there as an artist. His son and former wife live in Olympia, Washington.

My husband had also left the empty nest to accept a position with Lockheed Aircraft in Austin, Texas. In the good Marine wife tradition, I was to join him after I had sold the home and packed up the household goods. By 1985, having evolved with the times, I no longer identified with the persona of the dependent Marine wife, and freed from family responsibilities, I began a career search. Within two months, I was awarded a short-term technical writing assignment with Martin Marietta in Washington, D.C. working on their contract with the Federal Aviation Administration (FAA) to upgrade the National Airspace System.

At the end of this short-term assignment, Martin Marietta offered me a full-time position. It rendered me financially independent for the first time in our marriage and allowed me to make the physical separation from the children's father permanent. When Martin Marietta lost the contract 10 years later, the successor contractor, TRW, invited me to join them and carry on the work I had been doing for the FAA. I retired from TRW in 2001. The children's father retired from Lockheed and still lives in Austin, Texas. When we divorced in 1992, I legally adopted my Mother's maiden name to reclaim my Irish heritage and did not change it when I married Dennis W. Durham in 1996. We make our home in Alexandria, Virginia.

While there may be some who have never heard of the Cuban Missile Crisis, it had an enduring emotional impact on my life. Contemporary evidence indicates it also made an enduring impact both nationally and internationally. The world political scene remains fettered by embargos, although the U.S. Congress struck a deal in July 2000, which allowed food and medicine sales to Cuba. Fidel Castro's self-determination and sovereignty is still threatened by these embargos as well as other actions of the United States. His open and vocal distrust of "los yanquis" gives him his power.

The hope of improved conditions that swept Fidel Castro into power in the early 1960s has resulted in a wide generation gap in modern Cuba. State salaries are as low as $20 a month, and although old people still support Castro's "Revolutionary Army," today's Cuba offers nothing for the young.

Reported to be one of the major provocations of the 1962 Crisis, Castro still considers United States occupation of the Naval Base at Guantanamo Bay to be an immoral violation of his 'Patria'. In spite of the historical repercussions of doing so, the U.S. continues other provocations that Castro considers a violation of his sovereignty.

Each May there is talk of Cuban exiles in Washington and Miami toppling Castro. There are terrorists and saboteurs both within and without Cuba. Although the major organized effort of Cuban exiles, with U.S. help [the Bay of Pigs - April 1961] failed, exiles claim a different type operation is being planned, with not one large group, but many smaller groups.

The Elian Gonzales incident, while softening the Cuban dictatorship, did not bring about the sea change that was anticipated. Life in Cuba is such that attempted escape continues even under uncertain conditions. Thus, the unresolved debris of the Missile Crisis endures.

Oleg Troyanovsky, guest scholar from the Kennan Institute of the Woodrow Wilson Center for Scholars in Washington DC has said of the Cuban Missile Crisis:
It might perhaps be correct to say that never in history has any historical event assumed such great importance in all of its aspects, and been studied in such depth. I believe this is fully understandable, because never before had humankind been so close to the brink of nuclear holocaust.

We might all ask what changes in international behavior could avoid crises such as were experienced October 22, 1962 or September 11, 2001. Rollo May has said, "The paradox of being human is that we must be fully committed, but we must also be aware at the same time that we might possibly be wrong." [2] In recognition of this human paradox, Robert McNamara has said in some of the rebuttals about the Cuban Missile Crisis, "Human beings are fallible. We all make mistakes . . . we make them every day." [3]

Since Casto is committed to doing what he considers best for his people and Patria, and our current leaders are intent upon doing the same for us, this paradox allows the October 1962 crisis to continue. In the overall scheme of things, who is the victim in such a dilemma and who is the victor? What is the price?

Whenever I hear the strains of the Marine Corps Hymn, I am emotionally transported back to the paradox of that paradise. The Cuban Missile Crisis remains a symbol to me of all that is the best and the worst in any conflicted situation. The values, judgments, and motives of the key players are as similarly conflicted and subject to mistakes as the values, judgments, and motives of the average person.

We live in an age when survival is tenuous and events outrun our ability to make sense of them. With gratitude, we fasten onto news of the dignified, the brave, the gentle, and the intelligent, hoping to enhance each other's humanity. Obvious truths are lying in the open, begging to be amended before they are repeated. We feel pressured to make leading-edge automated decisions without losing our principles or individual human qualities? These contemporary issues somehow translate the global helix through which I lived into a universal problem, beset by the myriad complexities each individual faces in trying to live a life well.

---

[1]   James G. Blight, Bruce J. Allyn, & David A. Welch – Cuba on the Brink – Pantheon Books, NY – 1993, 48.
[2]   Rollo May – The Courage to Create – W. W. Norton & Company, NY/London – 1975, 20.
[3]   James G. Blight, Bruce J. Allyn, & David A. Welch – Cuba on the Brink – Pantheon Books, NY – 1993, 349.

#

Sketch Pad

THE WASHINGTON POST

TUESDAY, JANUARY 29, 2002

THE WASHINGTON POST

MONDAY, FEBRUARY 25, 2002   **A23**

Robert D. Novak

Marching Orders on Cuba

**For Cuba, the Crisis of October 1962 continues …
complete text of Novak editorial appears in Appendix.**

Appendix

Complete text of Robert D. Novak editorial from Washington Post February 25, 2002

Marching Orders on Cuba

Uruguay's President Jorge Batlle was engaged on Feb. 15 in a cordial Oval Office conversation with President George W. Bush, pledging his support for the war against terrorism, when the South American visitor hit a raw nerve. It would help the antiterrorist cause, said Batlle, if the United States ended its "blockade" of Cummunist Cuba.

Bush would have none of this. He told Batlle it is absolutely necessary to continue "what you call the blockade" – the long-standing U.S. trade sanctions against Cuba – so long as "that tyrant" continues his anti-democratic, anit-human rights rule. That tyrant is Fidel Castro.

The American president's outburst sets right some misconceptions in Havana, at the U.S. State Department and on Capitol Hill. The word has been spread that under Secretary of State Colin Powell's tutelage, Bush was going to seek normalization with Castro's dictatorial regime. While the trade embargo may be modified, it will continue and will no longer be the only instrument deployed by Washington to democratize Cuba. What's more, Powell is on board with an expanded anti-Castro strategy.

The Castro regime is so out of touch with this reality that Ambassador Vicki Huddleston, head of the U.S. Interests Section (in lieu of an embassy) in Havana was called into the Cuban Foreign Ministry the first week of February and given a dressing down. She was informed that she misrepresented the U.S. government a few days earlier when she said U.S.–Cuban relations would never improve unless and until Castro's harsh dictatorship softened.

Ironically, Huddleston was criticized by Cuban Americans for tilting toward Castro during the Clinton administration. Her attitude was transformed when Bush took the oath. Cuba's rulers are outraged that Huddleston's U.S. mission is violating censorship by distributing books, videotapes, audiotapes and cheap shortwave radios. Huddleston, a career foreign service officer, is merely following the old-fashioned professional diplomat's mandate to follow policies of the country's elected chief of government.

Other State Department careerists don't seem to understand that Clinton no longer is president. Jim Carragher, coordinator for Cuban affairs, and Ambassador John F. Maisto, special assistant to the president for Latin America, still lean toward rappoachement with an unreformed Cuba. Like-minded officials include Kevin Whitaker, deputy director of the Cuban desk, and his wife, Betsy, who works in public diplomacy.

Many of these officials believe presidents come and go, but Janice O'Connell lasts forevr. O'Connell is a veteran Senate Foreign Relations Committee staffer who (sponsored by Democratic Sen. Christopher Dodd of Connecticut) relentlessly presses for normalization with Castro. She approves personal service contracts by the U.S. mission in Cuba and recently warned a staffer there that his aggressive distribution of books and radios would get him kicked out of the country. She is particularly close to State Department lobbyist Maria Trejo, who is supposed to be representing the president's policies.

O'Connell was instrumental in stalling the installation of Bush's nominee as assistant secretary of state for Western Hemisphere affairs: Cuban-born Otto Reich. Disinformation was spread that Powell wanted to abandon Reich, but the president – backed by Powell – gave Reich a recess appointment. A new nomination of Reich will be sent to Congress, and ways will be found to keep him in a policymaking position if Senate Democratic leaders continue to deny him a vote.

Reich is now at work at the State Department working closely with Powell. An effective ally – Col. Emilio Gonzales, a former West Point professor – has been named to the National Security Council staff. Pro-Castro diplomats at the U.S. mission in Havana are about to be rotated elsewhere (though they are getting plum new assignments in Geneva and Lisbon, while Huddleston's next post is scheduled to be the less-than-popular Mali Embassy in Africa).

Castro's charm offensive is in full swing, wining and dining U.S. politicians in an effort to open the country to the U.S. trade and aid without Cuban democracy and human rights. President Bush is dedicated to preventing that, even if some foreign service officers do not yet realize it.

Copyright 2001, Creators Syndicate Inc.